NANJING
SUZHOU & WUXI

Caroline Courtauld

Rand McNally & Company
Chicago New York San Francisco

SBN 528-84349-4

Lib. of C. 80-54891

China Guides Series Limited
P.O. Box No. 31395
Causeway Bay Post Office
Hong Kong

The Gardens of Jiangsu by Maggie Keswick
Photographs by Magnus Bartlett,
represented by Woodfin Camp & Associates, New York
(2,7,8,17,25,49,54,61,66,69,70,73,89,96),
Caroline Courtauld (19,30,38,40,41,46,47,51,75,81,83,94),
Jill Hunt (78)
Editor: Jill Hunt   Map artwork: Arnold Wong
Design: Polygraphia Design & Production Ltd
Printed by The Wishing Printing Co. Ltd., Hong Kong

Contents

Map of Jiangsu Province 10
Jiangsu Province: 'Land of Fish and Rice' 11
The Gardens of Jiangsu by Maggie Keswick 13
Food in Jiangsu 21
Entertainment 23
The Grand Canal 26
Getting There 28
Climate and Clothing 29

Nanjing
Introduction 31
Hotels 32
Map of Nanjing 34
Restaurants 36
Shopping 37
Sights of Nanjing 39
Excursion to Yangzhou 52

Suzhou
Introduction 55
Map of Suzhou 56
Hotels 58
Restaurants 59
Shopping 60
Map of the Main Section of the Humble Administrator's
Garden 62
Gardens of Suzhou 64
Other Sights of Suzhou 67
Excursion to Changshu 74

Wuxi
Introduction 76
Hotels 76
Map of Wuxi 77
Restaurants 79
Shopping 80
Map of the Northeastern Shores of Tai Lake 80
Sights of Wuxi 81
Excursions from Wuxi 86

Recommended Reading 87
Useful Addresses 88
Index of Places 93
Chronology of Periods in Chinese History 95

For additional information on visas, custom formalities, health, money and communications, refer to **A Guide to All China** *published in this series.*

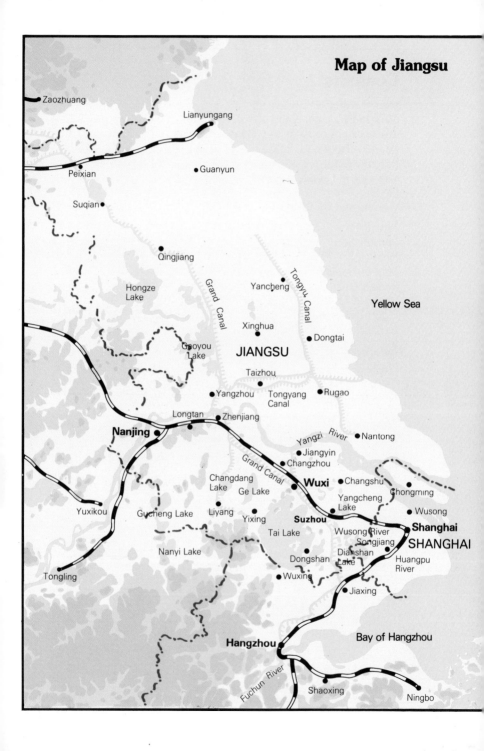

Jiangsu Province: 'Land of Fish and Rice'

Nanjing, Suzhou, Wuxi and Yangzhou are all to be found in the southern part of Jiangsu Province, China's 'Land of Fish and Rice'. Jiangsu is so called because, with its abundance of fertile soil and water, it is very rich in agricultural produce. Flowing through this flat plain, which is only relieved by a few hills to the west, is the vast Yangzi River. Over the centuries it has deposited rich alluvial soil on the land. At the river's mouth this silt has created natural land reclamation, which is still building up at the rate of three feet per year. As the eastern seaboard gradually bulged outwards, vast tracts of water were trapped forming lakes such as Hongze in the north, and Tai in the south. The fish and crustations caught in this transformation evolved into freshwater creatures. Indeed it was this process that gave rise to the region's premier delicacy, the Shanghai crab.

Jiangsu with 62 million people is the most densely populated province in China. The largest proportion of the population lives in Jiangnan, or southern Jiangsu, in which are also concentrated the major cities: Nanjing (the provincial capital), Suzhou and Yangzhou are ancient cities, Wuxi a modern industrial centre. (Shanghai is an independent municipality and now administratively outside the province.) These cities (together with Hangzhou in Zhejiang Province) are the major tourist spots of east China.

The richness of soil and abundance of water, as well as a temperate climate and mineral deposits, provided an ideal environment for the prosperous settlements that developed. All this rendered the region an attractive prize and by 600BC the Kingdoms of Wu, Yue and Chu were fighting for control of it — a struggle in which the King of Yue eventually triumphed. The wars of conquest continued, however. In the Han Dynasty (206BC-AD220) Jiangsu as we know it was made up of Yang and Xu Provinces. When the Han empire collapsed, the region became a part of the southern State of Wu, and began developing rapidly. More land was brought under cultivation by a series of irrigation and reclamation measures. The capital of the Southern Dynasties (420-589) — present-day Nanjing — grew in economic and cultural importance.

The fortunes of the province took a 'great leap forward' in the seventh century with the completion of the Grand Canal. Running from Luoyang (south of the Yellow River) the then capital, south through Yangzhou, Wuxi and Suzhou to

Hangzhou, this mammoth project provided China's first north-south trade route. It enabled the province to export to the less fertile north its food and the silk goods for which it had already become famous. Over these early centuries Nanjing acted as China's capital city during several different periods, Jiangsu being a pleasanter place to live than the cold barren north. (Nanjing momentarily fulfilled this role again in 1911 as the Republic of China's first capital, and again from 1928 to 1937.) However the constant fear of invasion meant that ultimately the capital had to be moved north.

Not only can the province boast fertile lands but also fertile minds. Lush, temperate Jiangsu proved attractive to scholars and poets, and colonies of wise men grew up in the region. They often served as senior administrators and government servants, and these 'Renaissance men' needed seclusion and a beautiful environment to pursue the contemplative, as opposed to the official, aspect of their life. This was the origin of many of the gardens of Suzhou and the surrounding area.

The modern cities of Jiangsu developed after the Treaty of Nanking (1842) which opened China to international trade. Since 1949 Jiangsu's economy has further expanded. The province maintains consistently high yields of its principal crops — rice, wheat, cotton — and its industries thrive.

Jiangsu, with its canalled cities, magnificent gardens and historical monuments, its placid lakes and great river, its traditional crafts, its legends and its astonishing food, offers the visitor a cornucopia of discovery.

The Gardens of Jiangsu

By Maggie Keswick

Gardening, like painting and ceramics, is one of the great arts of China. Yet, by the rest of the world it has been strangely neglected. We know something of Japanese gardens (which, incidentally, were originally inspired by a Chinese imperial park of the seventh century), and are aware of the terraced water-gardens of Moghul India. The gardens of France, Italy and England are famous. We are also reasonably familiar with Chinese painting and porcelain — not to mention Chinese poetry, sculpture, calligraphy and architecture (a branch of the arts very close to gardening). So how has it happened that Chinese *gardens* — which number among them some of the most fascinating in the world — have some-how been overlooked?

It is certainly not because making gardens is a new idea in China. We have the description of a garden in a poem that dates from the fourth century BC. In it, behind gauze silk curtains, doors of scarlet latticework lead out past winding streams to loggias, linked galleries and the scent of orchids on the breeze. High stepped terraces look across to distant hills, and balustrades lean out above a lake, its surface enamelled, beneath the blue-green umbrella leaves of summer lotus, with the purple stems of water mallows.

Perhaps this lovely place, with its delicate balance of natural streams and man-made pavilions, was as much a work of the imagination as the poem in which it appears. But the details are so precise it suggests the existence of real gardens from which the ancient poets drew their inspiration. Moreover, it stretches out across time like a premonition of what is to come: it could be describing a garden in China today.

If so, it would almost certainly be one of the gardens of Jiangsu, for, of all the provinces of China — from the mountain-ringed valleys of Chengde beyond the Great Wall, to the tropical lushness of Guangdong — none is more suited to the making of gardens.

Partly this is because Jiangsu has long been a land of plenty. Not only do its hills and streams lend themselves to garden design, but to agriculture: trees and flowers flourish, but fish and food crops too, and the prosperity they brought allowed a highly cultivated society to develop, producing in its turn many of China's most famous poets, painters, calligraphers and gardeners. Quite often these accomplishments were combined in a single person, for traditionally the Chinese felt that an educated man should be able to express his feelings by all these different means.

All the arts come together in the garden. Not only is it the nicest place in which to meet and paint or write poetry, but it also needs the eye of a painter both to create and appreciate it. As you walk around you will also see many poems that have been engraved on stone tablets and let into the walls — records of a pleasant day spent there by someone, perhaps a hundred years ago or more, who enjoyed just the same pavilions, scents and shadows as still are there today.

In this way a garden in China gradually acquires an extra dimension through time, for in an old and much-loved garden you feel close to the people who have known it in the past. Some of them have disappeared into obscurity, their names and feelings recorded nowhere else but on this single wall. Others are famous men, like the painter Wen Zhengming who lived and worked in the Suzhou Garden of the Humble Administrator. Up to the 1930s you could still see in that lovely place the wistaria he planted himself some 400 years before — or so they said. In any case, he may have thought up some of the names of the halls and pavilions — names subtly drawn from a poem by an earlier artist, perhaps, making yet another link with the past so that, interwoven with the sensuous sights and smells and sounds of the garden, are these gentle literary allusions — an appeal to the mind and the heart, as well as to the senses.

To a traditionally educated Chinese, this was what European gardens conspicuously lacked. Why, wondered one gentleman scholar — visiting England for the first time in the 1920s — why would one want a 'mown and bordered lawn, which, while no doubt of interest to a cow, offers nothing to the intellect of a human being?' Quite apart from the *mindlessness* of a lot of cut grass, his question brings up another point: for us a lawn is lovely because it is reminiscent — however distantly — of flower-studded pastures, of sweetness and peace in nature. But the Chinese are rice-growers, and to them cows and pastures suggest (if anything) hordes of barbarian, cattle-raising nomads riding across the northern borders to plunder the peaceful villages of Chinese farmers. In this case a lawn is not just incomprehensibly uneventful, but, across time, faintly but distinctly threatening.

The strange thing is, however, that when Chinese and English writers describe their gardens, they often sound almost interchangeable. Both of them see their gardens as 'natural' — particularly compared to those of their neighbours. The Chinese find Japanese gardens too mannered, too perfect, too composed to be natural. The English criticize French gardens for their 'unnatural' logic and geometry, forgetting that, to make Nature look the way they thought she should, they used just as much artifice as Le Notre. In fact gardens tell us a good deal about what each culture finds natural and it is not by any means always the same.

The 'naturalness' of Chinese gardens goes back to ancient times. In Europe, the first man to climb a mountain for the pleasure of looking out over untamed nature was Petrarch, in the 15th century. By that time the Chinese had been enjoying the delights of the wild for some 10 centuries or more. For Petrarch, initial feelings of awe and joy were overwhelmed by the idea that he had put Nature before God, and the beauty he had experienced suddenly became a temptation to sin. The Chinese had no such problems. Of their two main native philosophies, Confucianism concentrated on how man should live among men, while Daoism (Taoism) sought to discover how he should best fit into the great universe in which he lived. The *Dao* was made up of everything that exists — past, present and future — in its constant state of change and transformation. It was like a great seamless web of all creation, or the swirling patterns of mist in the mountains. Daoists aimed to fit so perfectly into these changing currents that they would become one with the forces of the *Dao*; death would become just another transformation, no more fearful than the sleep of a butterfly.

Daoists often opted out of organised society. But their philosophy, apparently so opposed to the Confucian emphasis on rites and duties, proved in time to be its necessary complement: Daoism provided a release from the constraints of being a 'superior man', and the Chinese (being practical people) found both philosophies valuable and applied them side by side — leaving the inconsistencies for foreigners to worry about. Thus the classic Chinese *house* with its symmetrical progression of courtyards may be seen as a symbol of the Confucian desire to regulate human relationships, while the Chinese *garden* — with its apparent disorder, its irregular, winding waterways, its rocky hills and loggias tucked into trees — mirrors the Daoist principle of harmony with nature. And, just as Daoism provided an acceptable escape from Confucian rectitude, so the design of a garden released the creative imagination which was allowed little scope in the planning of a house.

A Chinese garden, then, is ideally a retreat. It is — to borrow a Chinese phrase — a place to 'nourish the heart', where a man may tune himself to the rhythms of the natural world. But in case this sounds too solemn and highbrow, the Chinese garden is also a place of pure sensuous enjoyment, full of the scents of evening flowers. Though, like a Japanese garden, it was used for contemplation, the poetry competitions were often light-hearted affairs, full of teasing and laughter. And just as often gardens were the settings for parties, flower festivals, theatricals, lantern shows — and a little amorous dalliance. In China a retreat is hardly enjoyable without a few friends and a jar of wine.

In the 18th century, when justifying the expense of building a vast new garden, the Qianlong Emperor wrote that 'every emperor, when he has retired from audience and finished his public duties, must have a garden in which he may stroll, look around, and refresh his heart. If he has a suitable place in which to do this,' said he, 'it will regulate his emotions and relax his mind. If he has not, he will become engrossed in sensual pleasures and lose his will-power.' Since this was Qianlong's fourth great pleasure park, his subjects might have been excused a little scepticism. Nevertheless he had voiced a problem; from at least the fourth century (when a famously extravagant man built himself what he described as a 'simple country retreat') Chinese gardeners have wavered between the desire to conteract worldly vanities by the peaceful appreciation of simple nature — and the urge to indulge those very same vanities, in the setting of a luxurious pleasaunce.

It is true that all over the world gardens have been used to celebrate power and wealth (think of Versailles), but in China the great collections of plants and animals in the imperial parks gradually came specifically to symbolize all the variety of the empire. Exotic beasts from the icy north, birds from the tropical south, unknown trees from the mountains of the west — all these were sent to the emperor as tribute and set out in his hunting parks. There they testified to the magnificence and extent of the lands over which he ruled. And there too they gave rise to an idea that lies behind every Chinese garden —

that it should be a microcosm of the earth suggesting, even in a small space, all the riches of the universe.

It seems to me that this may be one of the reasons why Chinese gardens have been so little noted by the garden-makers of other countries. Like the Zen gardens of Japan they need some explanation for why they are so different from ours. In particular this applies to the density of China's old private gardens — the way in which so many effects are close-packed together, something that is a direct result of the desire to create a microcosm, often within the confines of an enclosed city garden.

It was for accessibility that many of China's old private gardens were in cities. 'If the heart is at peace,' wrote one scholar-official (trying to reconcile his Daoist love of freedom with his Confucian sense of duty) 'why should one not create a wilderness in the midst of town?' All that is needed is a high wall to close off the busy life outside, so the inside can be turned back again to nature. But to create, in a small space, the range of effects and emotions that might be experienced in a long country trip, requires extraordinary ingenuity.

So the Chinese garden designer created a labyrinth, in which the available space is layered by gateways and subdivided by walls that wind through the gardens with the regular undulations of sea-snakes or dragons. The whole garden becomes a composition of enclosed spaces. Some wind round corners out of sight. Others are open-ended. Some are cul-de-sacs, or fit into each other like pieces of a puzzle. And all of them are full of incident — winding lakes; bridges; pathways floored with pebble designs; moon-doors leading to halls; pavilions perched on giant rockeries; libraries, teahouses, galleries, terraces. High places lead to low, enclosed to open, shady to sunny, rocks to water, in a finely-tuned patterning of opposites. It is based, of course, on the ancient idea of yin/yang, those two opposing forces which the Chinese see underlying all creation. In practice, however, the result is almost magical. By leading you on through twisting galleries, by allowing the glimpse of a distant roof, by turning you back or making you pause for a moment, the Chinese designer managed to so confuse you that the space of his little garden seems to extend indefinately.

Yet it is in the intensity of the Chinese garden that the difficulty for foreigners chiefly arises. They were not, after all, meant to be seen in half a morning, but to be savoured over a

Garden of the Master of Fishing Nets, Suzhou

lifetime (and they often took a lifetime to make). For a woman with bound feet in old China, a garden (if she was lucky enough to have one) might be the extent of her universe. Small wonder if a quick tour round such a garden leaves new visitors with visual indigestion. Taken all in one gulp, a Chinese garden is a bewildering maze — and one seemingly more concerned with architecture than with growing things.

A foreigner's perplexity is intensified by extraordinary rocks. The gardens are full of them. Sometimes they are single, standing stones set up in much the same way we treat sculpture. Such pieces, billowing out from narrow bases, hollowed by water and time, pitted with holes and seemingly frozen in perpetual motion, are exceptionally powerful images. They may be seen as symbols of the *Dao* itself, but also of the boney structure of the earth. They may resemble lions or faces, and above all are regarded as aesthetic objects in their own right.

Even stranger, perhaps, are the huge piles of smaller rocks that the Chinese call 'false mountains'. These too loom massively into the courtyards, their peaks topped off with swooping-eaved pavilions, and their centres hollowed into caverns against the heavy summer heat. They are seen as the essential balance to water in the garden: their hard, pitted surfaces providing the *yang* principle to harmonize with the soft, reflective *yin* of the streams and lakes. In fact the Chinese phrase for 'landscape' is *shanshui* — meaning 'mountains-and-water': and one common way of saying 'make a garden' — literally translated means — 'heaping stones and digging waters'.

Such 'lakes' and 'mountains' also bring a sense of magic into the garden. Their origins lie in little islands once built by an emperor who hoped by them to lure the legendary Chinese Immortals into his garden. These Immortals lived on movable islands in the Eastern Sea, which forever dissolved into the mist as human travellers approached. The Immortals too could dissolve into the air, and fly about on the backs of storks — which made it difficult for the emperor to get hold of one to teach him the secrets of immortality. By building replicas of their magical habitations, the emperor hoped to confuse one into landing in his park, so that he might find out the truth. Though the emperor died at a perfectly normal age, in their rockeries Chinese gardens have kept alive, ever since, the memory of the island paradise of the Immortals.

Chinese gardens have a lot to teach us, not only in the skills of managing those small spaces which are increasingly to be our lot, but also in how to savour simple pleasures. What is so lovely about them is the way they can be enjoyed on many levels at the same time: despite the intoxicating beauty of Chinese gardens, their appeal is not only to the senses, but to the emotions too, and to the intellect. Behind the lovely shadows of the whitewashed walls, behind the sound of raindrops pattering on the summer lotus leaves, or the bright sparkle of reflected moonlight, there lies, for those who wish to find it, a profound and convincing view of the world, and of man's place in it.

Maggie Keswick is the author of **The Chinese Garden: History, Art and Architecture,** *published by Academy Editions, London, and Rizzoli, New York. She was born in Scotland and first went to China at the age of four. After school in Shanghai, Hong Kong and Surrey, England, she took an honours degree at Oxford, then studied at the Architectural Association in London. She is married to the critic and historian Charles Jencks, and they have two children.*

Food in Jiangsu

The food in Jiangsu is delicious, both the everyday and banquet varieties. If you have already sampled Shanghai cooking, then Jiangsu cooking techniques will be familiar. Dishes may be stir-fried, braised, steamed, fried in batter or marinated and grilled. Sauces are rich, heavier than in Cantonese cooking, and make extensive use of soy, ginger, sugar and Shaoxing wine.

The Land of Fish and Rice, Jiangsu produces an abundance of freshwater fish, crabs, shrimps and turtles, which form a focal point in any menu. Autumn is the season of the freshwater crab (sometimes called the Shanghai crab); if possible the visitor should sample this rich yet subtle flavour. When whole the crabs are steamed and then eaten by hand. First you break off and chew the hairy claws. Then, if the correct piece is pulled, seemingly by magic the crab falls in half exposing the succulent meat. As you eat it is customary to dip the crab into vinegar in which floats a little chopped ginger. Not only is this a complementary taste, but it is also supposed to cool the stomach. The rich crab meat is *yang* (male and heating); the vinegar *yin* (female and cooling). In Chinese culture, and thus cuisine, this balance between *yin* and *yang* is fundamental. After the crab is finished a hot ginger tea is served, again *yin* to cool the stomach and prevent indigestion.

Of the many varieties of fish, one of the most popular is the mandarin fish, which is served in a seemingly infinite number of ways. It is delicious, whether simply steamed, smothered with a hot spicy sauce or served as 'squirrel' fish, when it is first fried in sizzling oil and then served with a sauce that includes bamboo shoots, mushrooms, shrimps, ginger and onions. (When the sauce is poured over the fish, it makes the noise of a chattering squirrel.)

A wealth of mouthwatering specialities of the area awaits the visitor. There is the famous Beggar's Chicken — a dish whose origins are claimed by several Jiangsu towns as well as by Hangzhou — in which the chicken is wrapped in lotus leaves, encased in clay and baked in ashes. Spare ribs are another Jiangsu speciality, in a beancurd sauce in Wuxi or in a rich sweet and sour sauce in Suzhou. The well-known pressed duck of Nanjing, as well as the salt-cured duck, should also be sampled.

Dianxin (which literally means to dot the heart, to give the heart or more accurately the stomach a little pleasure) in this part of China covers a range of tasty morsels from delicate crescent shaped dumplings (*jiaozi*), steamed, fried or floated in clear soup, to cakes and pastries. A favourite sweet dish, eaten as a snack or as part of a banquet, is Eight-Treasure Rice — a cake of claret-coloured glutinous rice, red bean and pieces of crystallised fruit and nuts, over which a sauce is poured.

Unlike some other areas in China, where hotel food tends to be less exciting than in the restaurants outside, the hotels in Suzhou, Wuxi and Nanjing have excellent restaurants. Everyday cooking is good, and banquets which usually run to around 15 courses often prove to be the most memorable feasts in China.

Colour and texture at a Jiangsu banquet are very important: several dishes during a dinner will probably be served in the form of a picture — a bird, a basket of flowers, or perhaps a butterfly. These can be positively virtuoso creations: an ornate flower-basket of cold meats and patés as a first dish; or cranes in a landscape of gnarled trees (a familiar image in Chinese painting), their ruffled plumage depicted by delicately sliced layers of egg-white beneath which succulent chicken morsels give shape to their bodies; or to finish off the meal a large melon carved into the shape of a swan, filled with fruit.

Sweet dishes appear half way through the meal. These may be tiny intricate pastries filled with red bean paste, or brightly coloured dough sweets in the shapes of flowers, fruit or animals, or even sponge-cake made from green beans. Every banquet will include at least one dish exclusively of vegetables, such as a Three-coloured Vegetable dish or the exotic-sounding First Vegetable under Heaven.

Entertainment

Since 1978 Jiangsu, as everywhere in China, has experienced a great resurgence of the performing arts — traditional opera, both Chinese and western music, ballet, Chinese folk song and dance, and even western-style theatre. Although many of the companies to be seen in Jiangsu Province are based in Shanghai and from there tour the surrounding region, Nanjing, Wuxi and Suzhou also have their own troupes. Western visitors are most frequently taken to see acrobatics or to a variety show which offers a brief taste (sometimes incongruously mixed) of everything. Theatres are invariably packed, but seats can usually be found for foreign visitors. Yours CITS guide will tell you what is showing and get tickets for you.

For the Chinese, cinema is a favourite form of entertainment. Packed movie houses in the cities show Chinese and a growing range of western films (usually dubbed into Chinese). But most popular of all is still the traditional Chinese opera — a highly spectacular form of theatre combining music, song, dance, drama and acrobatics. In the old days all the lead parts in Peking opera were played by men, but today both actresses and female musicians perform. Some western theatre techniques have now been introduced. A tradition which is maintained however is that of using the staging of a particular opera to point a political message. Thus an opera telling the story of the first Qin emperor (221-210 BC) who forced scholars to travel north and help with the building of the Great Wall thereby risking death, alludes to the persecution of the educated during the Cultural Revolution.

There are also several types of opera native to Jiangsu Province. In the Ming Dynasty (1368-1644) a poetic style of drama, *Kunqu*, emerged in the south and became widespread. By the 16th century Suzhou had become the centre of this form, which used a soft flute as the main accompanying instrument. The music was more melodious, and movements and dialogue altogether lighter than the popular drama that originated in the north. One of the best known *Kunqu* operas is *Fifteen Strings of Cash*, which first appeared in the 17th century. Another is based on the story of Xi Shi's deception of the King of Wu (see under Yixing on page 86). The popularity of *Kunqu* declined in the 18th century and gave way to Peking Opera.

Yue Opera, founded in Shaoxing in the neighbouring province of Zhejiang at the end of the 1800s, is also popular in Jiangsu, since the inhabitants of northern Zhejiang, Suzhou, Wuxi and Shanghai all speak versions of the Wu dialect. Originally the show was for an all female cast, though today actors also take part. An adaptation of the *Dream of the Red Chamber* and of *Butterfly Lovers* are among the repertoire.

The most famous form of regional theatre is the Suzhou Ballad, which originated in the Tang Dynasty and reached the height of its popularity during Qing times. There are two types of Suzhou Ballad : one consisting purely of dialogue, usually of a historical nature, telling the tale of a famous hero or court case; the other, which incorporates some musical accompaniment, is based on love stories such as the *Story of the Three Smiles*. This form of theatre may not appeal to the foreign visitor for, unlike Peking Opera, there are no elaborate costumes, only one to three actors, no props other than perhaps a fan, a piece of wood and a *qin* (a long stringed musical instrument). The mood of the composition must be deduced from the eye movements and facial expressions of the actor, with which a truly great actor should be able to make his audience laugh or cry in quick succession. He must also be adept at producing his own special effects, such as a horse neighing or birds singing.

In Nanjing, to aid visitors' appreciation of opera, the enterprising local branch of CITS have concocted a simultaneous translation device.

The Grand Canal

'This enterprise, the greatest and most ancient of its kind, was found to extend from thence (Peking) to Hangchoo-foo (Hangzhou).' The Imperial or Grand Canal, thus described in the annals of Lord MacCartney's 1793 Embassy to China, remains the largest man-made waterway in the world.

Yang Di, the second emperor of the Sui Dynasty (581-618), started building the Grand Canal in 605. Yang Qian his father had successfully reunited China, following the ravages of 400 years of the chaotic Warring States period, and made his capital at Changan (Xi'an) in the north. To his sons he gave official posts throughout the country, and his second son Yang Di became Viceroy of Jiangdu (modern Yangzhou). Yang Di's task of eradicating the southern hatred and suspicion for his father's new dynasty throughout what is today Jiangsu Province was a mammoth one. This he achieved with great personal sophistication. He married a well-born girl from Nanjing, a descendant of the former Liang Dynasty, who not only taught him the local Wu dialect but introduced him to the southern ways. Yangdi surrounded himself with eminent scholars both religious and secular, rebuilt temples and generally lived the life that was expected of an aesthete and southern prince.

On his father's death in 605 Yang Di ascended the throne, having first overthrown his elder brother. Then began what has made Yang Di's name famous throughout Chinese history, his canal building. He returned to the northern capital and very soon began this 'work of no less genius than material utility', the building of the Grand Canal. The reasons for this canal system — the Grand Canal was one of a network of canals — were various. First, both the capital Changan (Xi'an) and also Luoyang, the new capital under construction, were situated in a dry, food-deficient area, a situation which the increasing population would further exacerbate. Thus the canal was necessary for importing grain. Secondly, to sustain the reunification of China the canal was essential for rapid troop movements. Thirdly, the emperor felt that the wealth and majesty of the dynasty should be displayed nationwide.

The construction of the Grand Canal took only a small proportion of Yang Di's 13-year reign. This was possible mainly because it followed the course of earlier Han canals, and also because it was built along a flat alluvial plain — there are few locks as it is generally fed by rivers. A contemporary Sui historian tells us that to build the stretch from the Huai River (in the north of Jiangsu Province) to Yangzhou, the emperor mobilised a hundred thousand workers — both men and women — and for the northern stretches, 9 million workers. Not only, Sir George Staunton (Lord MacCartney's chronicler) tells us, did the canal have to be dredged and cut between 60 and 100 yards across in some places, its banks faced with stone, but also it was bordered by imperial tree-lined roads and tow paths. 'Solid and permanent bridges are thrown over the canal in many parts . . . . . some of coarse grey marble'.

An imperial journey from Luoyang down the canal to Yangzhou is thus described in a contemporary treatise on economics. 'Boatmen hired from all the waterways . . . . pulled the vessels by ropes of green silk. The emperor rode in a dragon boat. The boats followed one another poop to prow for more than 200 leagues' (about 65 miles). When, in 616, opposition to his rule became too violent in the north of his empire, Yang Di set off down his Grand Canal to seek refuge in Yangzhou, where he remained until his murder in 618 put an end to the Sui Dynasty. Both contemporary historians and others down to the present day have been hard on Yang Di. Certainly during his last years he devoted himself to debauching and cared little for the well-being of his empire and subjects. However, the importance of his legacy of the Grand Canal cannot be understated and much of the prosperity of the following Tang Dynasty is attributable to it.

By the time of Marco Polo's extended visit to China in the 13th century the 'Grain Canal' as it became known was 'Khubilai Khan's glory'. In fact all was well with the canal until the 1850s when, we are told by the chronicler of Lord Elgin's 1857-59 journeys, sections 'of that once celebrated channel of internal commerce of the empire were destroyed by the flooding Yellow River; the consequence is, that the enormous Imperial Grain junks formerly employed now line the bank in a rotting condition. They are singular specimens of natural architecture, of immense solidity, and capable of transporting from two to three hundred tons of rice each'. Despite this problem the canal around Suzhou, Wuxi and Yangzhou was always and remains extremely busy. Laurence Oliphant, the private secretary to Lord Elgin's 1857 Embassy to China, presents us with vivid descriptions. 'There are as many different varieties of boats here as there are of vehicles in Fleet Street and the waterway was as inconveniently crowded as that celebrated thoroughfare usually is . . . . Gentlemen's private carriages were here represented by gorgeous mandarin-junks, with a huge umbrella on the top, and a gong at the entrance to the cabin, beaten at intervals by calfless flunkes. . . . . But the most curious appearance was presented by the boats which carried fishing cormorants. Solemnly perched in successive rows on stages projecting from the sides, they looked like a number of gentlemen in black on the platform at a meeting of a grave and serious matter.' There is even a mention of the courtesan or flower boats: 'other junks there were, more gaudily painted even than these from whence issued shrill voices and sounds of noisy laughter and music'.

Today gone are the mandarin-junks, flower boats and regal imperial processions, but the Grand Canal is still a living, bustling thoroughfare, transporting produce from the Land of Fish and Rice to the north. However, many of the craft are probably little different from those plying the waterway in previous centuries: the cormorant boats are still to be seen, basic wooden barges strung together in long lines, making their slow progress more often than not powered by pole. The Grand or Imperial Canal constructed over 1300 years ago is still serving its main original purpose.

Getting There

By air

At present there are no direct flights to Nanjing from outside China, so passengers travelling from Hong Kong have to change in Canton. In addition there are daily Shanghai/Nanjing and Peking/Nanjing flights. Wuxi and Suzhou have no airport.

By rail and road

Nanjing The 1314-mile rail journey from Canton to Nanjing takes 30-40 hours. Sleeping cars in China are very clean and comfortable and the dining car food is acceptable. Trains to Nanjing from Wuxi take 2½ hours, from Shanghai 4½ hours, from Suzhou 3¼ hours and the sleeper from Peking roughly 18 hours.

Suzhou From Shanghai the train journey takes 1½ hours, from Wuxi 45 minutes, from Hangzhou 4 hours and from Nanjing 3½ hours. By taxi or coach: the ride from Wuxi to Suzhou takes 1¼ hours on a poor road, though through attractive farmland. Shanghai is 2½ hours by road, also an interesting drive.

Wuxi By rail the journey from Nanjing takes 2½ hours, from Shanghai just under 2 hours and from Suzhou 40 minutes. By taxi or coach — the 42 miles from Suzhou, along a poorly surfaced road, takes 1¼ hours.

It is now possible for tourists to travel by boat on some sections of the Grand Canal. The boat journey between Wuxi and Suzhou, which takes about 3½ hours, is an attractive alternative means of transport now included in some tour itineraries.

Climate and Clothing

Nanjing, Suzhou and Wuxi all have similiar climates. The pleasantest seasons to visit them are spring and autumn when the days should be dry, sunny and warm, the evenings cool — so it is advisable to take a sweater. Their winter months are cold with temperatures sometimes falling to -7°C (17°F) with occasional snow. In common with elsewhere in China the Jiangsu Province hotels have very powerful central heating, but it is essential to take plenty of warm outdoor clothing. The local stores supply a good selection of cashmeres, fur hats and fur-lined padded coats for the cold or ill-equipped traveller.

The rainy season is during May, when mackintoshes and umbrellas are indispensable. The weather in Wuxi, due to its proximity to Tai Lake and intersection by the Grand Canal, is always fairly damp and misty: umbrellas should at all times be near at hand. On a dank day the local people can be seen hurrying along under magnificent king-size yellow oilskin ones.

Jiangsu summers tend to be hot and humid, the July temperature rising to 36°C (97°F). Due to the 24 million trees that were planted after Liberation, Nanjing is no longer one of 'the three furnaces of China', and its summer temperatures have dropped into line with those of Wuxi and Suzhou. Most of the hotels have some form of airconditioning but very few of the places you may visit do, so only thin clothes are required in summer.

Nanjing

Introduction

Nanjing, the capital of Jiangsu Province and today a city of three million people, has a long and complex history. The first settlements were recorded in the Spring and Autumn Period (770-476BC). From the beginnings of the Six Dynasties (220-589), when Nanjing was the cultural centre of China, it was several times the capital. Poetry and painting flourished during this time: many literati, such as the poet Li Bai (Li Po, 701-762), lived here. The city was again prominent in the Southern Tang (937-75). By the time of the Southern Song (1127-1279) it had become a commercial as well as an artistic centre, and was also renowned for its flower boats filled with desirable courtesans along the Qinhuai River. Early in its history a writer likened Nanjing to 'a dragon curling and tiger crouching': its Purple Gold Mountains 'tiger crouching' to the east, and the Yangzi River 'dragon curling' round the city to the west.

The first Ming emperor Zhu Yuanzhang made Nanjing his capital in 1368. With the lure of high office and honours he persuaded (it is said) 20,000 rich families to make it their home and contribute towards the city. It took Zhu Yuanzhang or the Hongwu Emperor (his reign title) 18 years and the labours of over 200,000 men to complete his 50-square mile city. In 1421, Zhu Yuanzhang's son, the Yongle Emperor, moved the capital back to Peking, and the city was renamed Nanjing, or Southern Capital. But Nanjing continued to prosper, with the growth of industries such as weaving and shipbuilding. The Sanchahe Yards built the ships for the historic journeys of the eunuch Admiral Zheng He (1405-33) to the Indian Ocean and Africa. Also Nanjing continued to be a centre of scholarship.

In 1842 the Treaty of Nanjing was signed, ending the first Anglo-Chinese Opium War and marking the opening of five Treaty Ports to the west. In the first half of the 19th century a revolutionary tradition developed in Nanjing. In 1853 it became the capital of the Taiping Rebellion. Then in 1911 Dr Sun Yat-sen established the first Republican government there. Subsequently Nanjing was controlled by warlords until the Guomingdang (Nationalist Party) made Nanjing the capital of a united China once more in 1928. During the Sino-

Japanese War Nanjing fell to the Japanese in 1937 and Chiang Kai-shek moved his capital to Chongqing. In the sack of the abandoned capital, 100,000 citizens were massacred by the Japanese. The atrocities came to be known as the 'Rape of Nanking'. Nanjing was liberated in April 1949 by Mao Tse-tung. He declared at the time, quoting the ancient writer, 'the city a tiger crouching, a dragon curling outshines its ancient glories; in heroic triumph heaven and earth have been overturned'.

Today portions of the original city wall stand and the boulevards, once paved with the Emperor Hongwu's marble, are still the main arteries of the city. These are impressive affairs consisting of two main traffic lanes, two more for bicycles, four pavements for pedestrians and the whole shaded by no less than four lines of graceful plane trees. They are alive with honking horns and chirping bicycle bells: the constant noise providing this vast, vibrant city with an uninterrupted, early morning quality.

There are 2000 industrial and mining enterprises in Nanjing as well as 40 hospitals, 1500 primary schools and 15 universities and institutions of higher learning.

Since 1949 Nanjing, once one of the three furnaces of China (so called because of unbearably high summer temperatures), has become a cooler place, physically as well as politically, in which to live. The planting of 24 million trees (part of a nationwide campaign inspired by Mao) has lowered the summer temperature by three to four degrees centigrade. The trees also help to reduce pollution and of course beautify the city. 18 parks surround the city, the largest of which, Xuanwu, is almost 1000 acres.

Hotels

南京饭店　中山北路259号
NANJING HOTEL 259 Zhongshan Road North tel. 34121
Nanjing Hotel is set in a spacious walled garden with lawns and a sweeping driveway, near the centre of the city. Like many hotels in China, it is made up of several buildings with construction dates spanning some 30 years. The Russian-built section, put up in the '50s, has sombre guest rooms, spacious but a little shabby, with long dark corridors and wide staircases. The restaurant, whose high ceilings can make eating uncomfortably cold in winter, is reached by walking across the garden. A new restaurant is scheduled to open soon.

双门楼宾馆   双门楼38号 *Westayed*
SHUANGMENLOU GUESTHOUSE 38 Shuangmenlou
tel. 85622
Eight buildings make up this hotel, the oldest dating from the
turn of the century. Until the Japanese occupation it was the
British Consulate. The total complex has 200 rooms each with
a private bath, but the quality of accommodation varies
considerably from building to building. There are two dining
rooms serving good Chinese food and also some western
dishes. Excellent banquets are given in the elegant old
panelled dining rooms of the former British Consulate.

丁山宾馆   察合尔路90号
DINGSHAN GUESTHOUSE 90 Qahar Road tel. 85930
On a hill overlooking the city, this eight-storey Chinese built
hotel was opened in 1978. In 1980 a new section was added,
made up of several two-storey prefabricated buildings,
expanding the hotel's capacity to 357 rooms with baths. The
prefabricated units, imported into China by an Australian-
based Overseas Chinese company and assembled by Australian
contractors, were the first hotel buildings put up with foreign
co-operation to be completed. Although the rooms are small,
airconditioning in summer and effective heating in winter are
particularly welcome.

东郊宾馆   陵园路5号
EAST SUBURB GUESTHOUSE 5 Lingyuan Road
tel. 41700
This guesthouse comprises a cluster of low buildings, providing
some 50 bedrooms with bathrooms en suite. The spacious
dining rooms are in a separate building. What distinguishes this
guesthouse from the other accommodation offered in Nanjing
is its superb location. Near the Ming Tomb, east of the city
centre, it is set in a secluded, wooded compound which were
the grounds of Chiang Kai-shek's Nanjing country residence.
The post-1949 guesthouse was used for state visitors to the
People's Republic.

胜利饭店   中山路76号
VICTORY HOTEL 76 Zhongshan Road tel. 42217
This is the only centrally located hotel. The entire hotel dates
from the 1920s and the rooms (45 in all) are more basic than
those of the other hotels; for example, they do not have
private baths. It has two excellent restaurants, a coffee shop
and a craft shop.

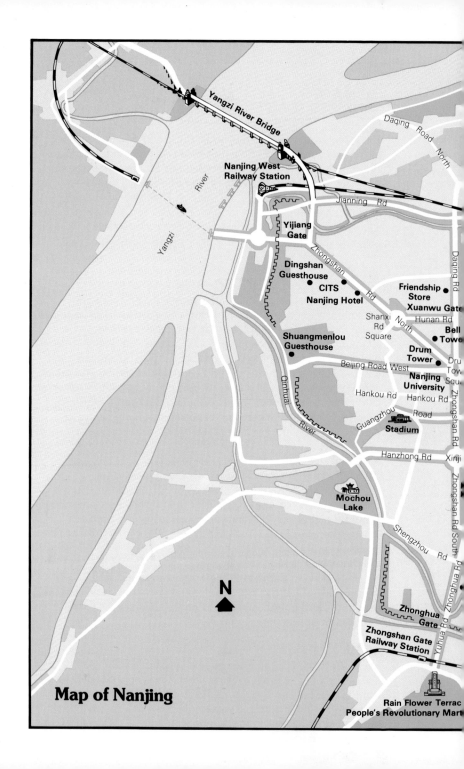

Map of Nanjing

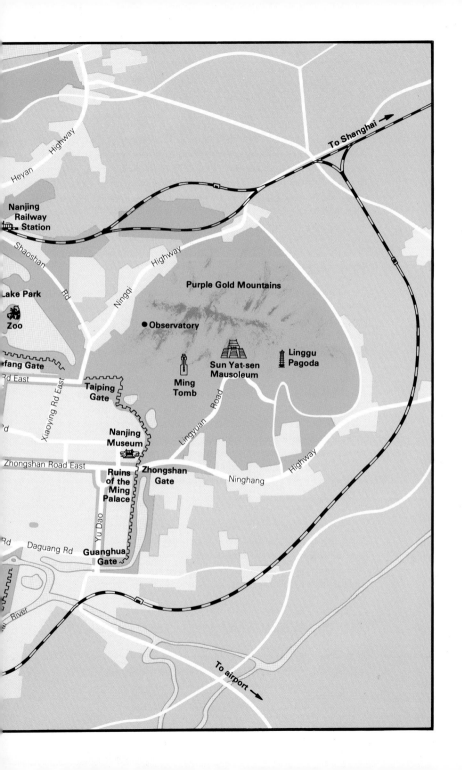

金陵饭店　中山路 5 号
JINLING HOTEL 5 Zhongshan Road
Work on this hotel, which is being built with foreign co-operation, began in March 1980. In the centre of Nanjing, the hotel is to be 36 storeys, topped by a revolving restaurant. The hotel will be able to house 1500 guests in 804 rooms. Plans for the building include a large coffee shop, swimming pool and other facilities expected of an international standard hotel. The Jinling is expected to open at the end of 1982, and as such will be the first full-scale hotel built with foreign co-operation to be completed in modern China.

Restaurants

The food in the restaurants of the three biggest hotels can be excellent. Instead of having their daily set menu try some regional specialities: walnut duck, abalone and pigeon soup, or mandarin fish with shrimp stuffing. The chocolate soufflé at Nanjing Hotel is a triumph — it is served in individual dishes and is all that soufflé lovers dream of. It must be ordered in advance.

The smaller Victory Hotel has two fine restaurants, Chinese and western. Duck is a speciality, particularly cold pressed duck — a typical Nanjing dish. Also try turtle casserole, and sugared walnuts. A new icecream parlour at the Victory is a lively room decorated with neon signs. Uncharacteristically one sits looking through an uncurtained picture window onto the street. Many flavours of icecream (including 'mandarin' and 'cream coke') as well as pastries and drinks are served.

Outside the hotels, as would be expected of a major city, there are many restaurants offering not only Nanjing specialities but also a range of other kinds of Chinese cuisine. The following restaurants, which have not been visited by the author, are also open to tourists:

江苏酒家　健康路126 号
JIANGSU RESTAURANT 126 Jiankang Road tel. 23698

回族饭店　中山路
MOSLEM RESTAURANT Zhongshan Road tel. 33807

老广东菜馆　中山路45号
OLD CANTONESE RESTAURANT 45 Zhongshan Road
tel. 42482

北京羊肉馆　中山东路94号
PEKING MUTTON RESTAURANT 94 Zhongshan Road East
tel. 42585

四川饭店　太平路171号
SICHUAN RESTAURANT 171 Taiping Road tel. 43651

缘柳居素茅馆　太平南路246号
LULIUJU VEGETARIAN RESTAURANT 246 Taiping Road
South tel. 43644

Shopping

Nanjing has plenty to offer the keen shopper. There are
several department stores, the largest of which, Renmin
Bazaar, is in Zhongshan Road. It is a bustling Aladdin's Cave
filled with treasures both to look at and to buy: a whole room
of enamelware, for the brave locally made herbal face cream
sold in the dollop from large sweet jars, 'fashion' knitwear, gay
childrens' clothes, linen, vivid longjohns and even washing
machines and televisions.

Several minutes' walk away at 199 Zhongshan Road is the
Nanjing Gallery which shows and sells the work of local artists
and also reproductions. Next door is an art shop selling
brushes, seals, fans, rubbings and slides of local scenery.
Opposite is a noodle shop where, if you are lucky, you can
see noodle dough being kneaded and thrown.

Away from this hurly-burly is a sober Friendship Store at 3
Daqing Road, two antique shops, a small one at the Nanjing
Museum, the larger better-stocked one at 7-11 Hanzhong
Road. At 168 Xinjiekou there is an Arts and Crafts Store, and
the Foreign Languages Bookstore (Waiwen Shudian) is a good
book, map and poster shop.

Sights of Nanjing

The Ming Tomb

To the east of the city towards the Purple Gold Mountains lies the Ming Tomb. The founder of the Ming Dynasty, the Emperor Hongwu, who died in 1392, is buried there with his empress. If you leave the city through the Zhongshan Gate the road follows the old Ming city wall — much of the original 35 miles stands today — thus bringing you to the start of the sacred way which leads to the tomb. Along the sacred way are 12 pairs of stone animals alternately standing and lying and, at the far end, stone military and civil servants. In comparison to the later more renowned sacred way at the Ming Tombs near Peking, this is in a beautiful setting surrounded by wooded hills and has a charming intimate feeling. Instead of the animals lining both sides of a busy tarmac road, these magnificent statues are barely 10 feet apart under the shade of mature trees. The path through the middle is used by an occasional bicyclist, the animals as shelter by picnicking children, and on either side of this fine avenue runs a small road. Little remains of the mausoleum itself, save a stone gate and a courtyard, which was plundered during the Taiping Rebellion.

Sun Yat-sen Mausoleum

Dr Sun Yat-sen is often called the Father of modern China. In 1911 he and his Guomindang (Nationalist Party) overthrew the Qing, the last imperial dynasty of China. On 1st January 1912 they established the first Republican government in Nanjing. Dr Sun died in Peking in 1925 and in 1929 his ashes were moved to the newly finished mausoleum, partially financed by donations from Overseas Chinese. The white buildings, with roofs of brilliant blue tiles (the two colours of the Guomindang flag) stand out from their background of sombre green wooded hills. The memorial hall itself is approached up a wide flight of 392 granite steps. A large seated statue of Dr Sun by the French sculptor Landowski dominates the hall. On the walls are extracts from the 1912 constitution. Leading off from the hall is a small circular building which contains the tomb, on top of which is a marble statue of Dr Sun in death.

Linggu Temple Park

East of the Sun Yat-sen Mausoleum lies Linggu Temple Park, which contains two interesting buildings — Wuliangdian (Without Beams) and a 200-foot high pagoda. Wuliangdian, a brick structure of the Ming Dynasty (1368-1644) was built over a huge mud mound which was then hollowed out leaving a vast vaulted hall, thus using no wood. Also of structural interest is that sticky rice was used for the pointing. Muslim eunuchs from the court used to worship here. It was also used as a classics reading room, a prayer book store and, above the dais, the results of the civil service examinations were posted. Behind Wuliangdian stands the nine-storey pagoda which was rebuilt by the Guomindang in 1929. For the energetic the long climb to the top is rewarded with a fine view over wooded countryside.

The Observatory

The Nanjing Observatory is on the third peak of the tree-clad Purple Gold Mountains to the northeast of the city. It was founded in 1934 and is now the third largest observatory in China: 200 scientists are based there. There is a small collection of Ming copies of earlier astronomical instruments, a Han celestial globe, an ancillary sphere for detecting solar bodies, a Zhou Dynasty gnomon (sun and seasons dial) and an earthquake detector first made in the Warring States period (476-221BC). The recent histories of these last two instruments have been disturbed: in the early 1930s the Japanese tried unsuccessfully to remove the gnomon; they even cut the base in half. In the 1900s the Germans absconded with the earthquake detector, but it was returned to Nanjing in 1935. Climb onto the platform roof of one of the observatory domes and you will find yourself above the tree line and, unfurling below you, a marvellous view of Nanjing and the 'dragon curling' Yangzi.

Yangzi River Bridge

It is with considerable pride that the tourist is shown the giant Yangzi Bridge, the nearest point to the sea that the great river is spanned. It provides a vital link between the north of China and the rice bowl of the south. Before the bridge was completed in 1968, all traffic had to cross the swirling river by

(Preceding page) Sun Yat-sen Mausoleum, Nanjing

ferry. Today, one is told, some 160 trains and 10,000 vehicles cross daily. Construction began in 1960 and took an estimated 7000 workers, consumed 100,000 tons of steel and cost a total of 280 million *yuan* (roughly US$200 million).

When the concept of the bridge was born the Soviet Union agreed to supply the majority of the steel and the design and engineering expertise. However, they later withdrew and, with remarkable resourcefulness, the Chinese not only designed the almost four-mile bridge themselves but also revamped the domestic steel industry to produce the required tonnage.

At either end of the bridge stand four towers. In one of these is housed the visitor's briefing room and a fine model of the bridge. The Yangzi River Bridge is two-tiered, the top level for vehicles, the lower one for trains. To visit the railway deck and look along the great grey tunnel of steel is awe-inspiring, especially so if one of the massive steam engines thunders past. There is an equally impressive view from the top of the visitor's tower: from this vantage point one can appreciate the scale of the achievement involved in spanning these turbulent waters.

Rain Flower Terrace and People's Revolutionary Martyrs' Memorial

To the south of the city lies the Rain Flower Terrace, or Yuhuatai. Formerly a place of Buddhist pilgrimage, today it is where the famous pebbles of Nanjing are collected. Legend has it that the terrace is so named because in the Liang Dynasty (502-557) the preaching of a monk named Yun Guang so pleased the Lord Buddha that the rain which fell was like flowers which then turned into agate pebbles. Since the Qing Dynasty the terrace has been the site of numerous executions, and today the visitor can see a memorial erected after Liberation to commemorate the 100,000 revolutionaries the Guomindang executed there between 1927 and 1949. If possible visit the terrace after rain: the pebbles glisten and become translucent.

Stone Carvings of the Southern Dynasties

One hour's drive north of the city, scattered among the paddy fields, stand groups of gigantic Liang Dynasty (502-557) stone animals. These mythical creatures mark the entrances to the tombs of 11 emperors and 20 princes and noblemen, the best preserved being those in front of the tombs of the Emperor Wen and of Prince Kang.

Ruins of the Ming Palace

The Ming Palace was built in 1368 by Hongwu, the first emperor of the Ming Dynasty. Hongwu was born a peasant. At the age of 17, so the story goes, after a plague of locusts had left him orphaned and destitute, he became a monk so as to beg for food. Later, when he saw the Mongol Yuan Dynasty crumbling, he joined and then took command of the rebel army. After 13 years of fierce fighting he ejected the Mongols from China. He then returned south and chose Nanjing to be his capital. Today, little of the former palace remains except the bases of the five marble bridges and some foundations of three vast Halls of Audience. The palace was burnt by Hongwu's son Zhu Di when fighting to capture the throne from his nephew, Hongwu's grandson and the second Ming emperor. Victorious, Zhu Di, or Yongle (his reign title as the third Ming emperor) moved his capital back to Peking where he built the Imperial Palace that survives today, using many of his father's plans from the Nanjing palace.

Museum of the Taiping Heavenly Kingdom

The Treaty of Nanking in 1842 opened China's doors to western powers and accelerated the decline of the Qing government. The treaty terms and evidence of Qing misgovernment caused widespread social unrest, particularly in the southern provinces. In 1851 Hong Xiuquan, leading peasant rebels, declared a new state named Taiping Tianguo (Heavenly Kingdom of Peace) in Guangxi. The Taiping cause was anti-Manchu, opposed to traditional culture and institutions, and inspired by religious ideas that were tinged with Christianity. Hong Xiuquan and his followers captured Nanjing in 1853 and made it their Celestial Capital. The Taiping uprising was finally suppressed by the Manchus, but Nanjing suffered great devastation during the conflict.

The Museum of the Taiping Heavenly Kingdom is housed in the former palatial residence of a Ming mandarin. During the Heavenly Kingdom it was used by Hong Xiuquan's assistant. The museum shows a detailed history of the Taiping movement from 1848 to the fall of Nanjing in 1864. In the attractive garden is a well-preserved marble boat.

Memorial Hall of the Delegation of the Chinese Communist Party

Numbers 17, 30 and 35 Mei Garden New Road are the buildings where Premier Zhou Enlai lived and made the headquarters of the Chinese Communist Party during negotiations with the Guomindang in 1946 and 1947 at the end of the Sino-Japanese War. The austere headquarters and the charming house and garden are as Zhou Enlai is said to have left them: Palgrave's *Dictionary of Political Economy* on the shelf, clothes in the cupboard, Nanjing pebbles on the sitting room table, a highly polished two-tone green and beige Chrysler in the garage. The peepholes through which the Guomindang spied on the Chinese Communist Party are shown to the visitor.

Drum Tower and Bell Pavilion

At either side of one of the main crossroads of the city, stand two fine Ming buildings, the Drum Tower (Gulou) and the Bell Pavilion (Dazhongting). They are under restoration and so closed to visitors for the time being (1980).

Nanjing Museum

The Nanjing Museum was opened in 1933: it is well laid out, with six large exhibition halls. Its exhibits date from the Western Zhou Dynasty (around 11th century-770BC) up until 1919. One of the most interesting is a jade burial suit dating from the Eastern Han Dynasty (25BC-220AD). This would have belonged to an official of high rank. It was unearthed in Jiangsu Province in 1970 and is made of 2000 rectangles of green jade sewn together with 800 grammes of silver thread. The jade suit totally encapsulated the body with the object of preserving it. But when archaeologists dug it up all they discovered inside were bones.

The early bronze section contains coins (with square holes in the middle) and weights and measures dating from the first Qin emperor (221-210BC) Elsewhere you will find a delightful collection of what is apparently doll's house furniture: in fact they are burial objects made in 1456 for a Ming mandarin, the custom being to be buried with miniature copies of your worldly goods to help with your afterlife. Perhaps the most fascinating exhibit of all is the larger-than-life bronze statue of a man, said to date from the Warring States (475-221BC), with all the acupuncture points on the body. Another reminder of China's superiority in early medical pioneering is a portrait of Hua To (141-203), a doctor and acupuncturist and reputedly the first man to employ anaesthesia.

The museum is filled with many other interesting exhibits and is well worth an extended visit. It also has a shop selling good reproductions and knick-knacks plus a separate antique shop. The museum's conservation department is researching, among other things, new methods to prevent dehydration of lacquer and wooden objects and protection of silk against mildew.

Zhonghua Gate, Nanjing

Zhonghua Gate

In 1866 a visitor mentioned 'passing through the high gates, under a tunnel at least a 100 feet long' — an entrance into Nanjing one can repeat today and find the Zhonghua Gate in excellent repair. Built in 1368, it was originally called Collected Treasure Gate. It is a square structure of three

15-foot walls and courtyards with vaulted gates in the middle of each wall. Guards and cavalry were housed in the ample walls. This is by far the most interesting and best preserved gate, with an excellent view of the Qinhuai River and the city from the top of its ramparts.

Travelling around Nanjing you will see the remaining gates — all much smaller affairs, they are only one arch deep. They include Xuanwu, west of the lake by the same name, Taiping to the northeast, Zhongshan to the east, and Yijiang to the northwest. Most are linked to the city wall though Zhongshan Gate majestically straddles a dual carriageway.

Xuanwu Park

To the northeast of the city through the Xuanwu Gate lies the largest of Nanjing's 18 parks, Xuanwu — it is roughly seven square miles. This beautiful park, ringed by hills with the Purple Gold Mountains to the east, was laid out in the 1900s. It was given a facelift in the 1950s when several facilities were added such as an ice rink, an open-air theatre, a children's playground and an excellent zoo showing both the giant black and white pandas and the small yellow, or lesser pandas. The park's large lake is straddled by five islets linked by stone bridges and causeways which people use in summer to visit the fragrant lotus beds.

Nanjing University

Foreign tour groups are sometimes taken to visit the university, where students from the English department act as enthusiastic hosts.

Of the 15 institutions of higher education in Nanjing, Nanjing University is the most renowned and the largest. It was founded in 1902 and since its post-Liberation expansion has produced 20,000 graduates. It boasts 12 departments in the arts and sciences with 41 specialities, a fine library of two million books as well as a farm and three factories. Each year the University accepts a certain number of overseas students as well as several visiting professors.

Mochou Lake

Outside the western city wall, this pleasure ground of pavilions, causeways and an open-air theatre built round a lake provides a perfect retreat from the city. It was laid out in the

Song Dynasty. Its name means 'light-hearted' and com-
memorates the life of a popular Liang Dynasty heroine and the
resilience with which she faced many tribulations. Gradually
over the years the pavilions fell into disrepair and the lake
silted up, with the result that major restoration work was
required in the 1950s. The Shengqi Pavilion with its Ming
foundations, and the Yujin Hall were rebuilt, and bamboo
groves, the Lotus Water Terrace and cherry-apple gardens
have been planted.

Qixia Temple

For visitors spending more than a few days in Nanjing, a
visit to Qixia Temple and the Thousand Buddha Cliff is
strongly recommended. They are situated 12 miles from the
stone carvings of the Southern Dynasties. The temple, which
was originally built in 487, and restored under the Tang and
Yuan, is still inhabited by monks, and boasts an exceptional
library of 7200 volumes. One of the buildings standing beside
this temple is a six-storey octagonal pagoda, built under the
Sui Dynasty (581-618) which has an interesting carved base.
Near the pagoda is the Thousand Buddha Cliff. In each niche
of the cliff is a sculpture, the oldest dating from the Qi (one of
the Southern Dynasties). This was the period when Buddhism

On a Jiangsu canal

was beginning to take a hold in Jiangsu Province: many temples were built and these rock sculptures were part of this religious expansion.

Nanjing's Silk Industry

Nanjing has three silk factories producing many kinds of cloth but specialising in *yunjin*. The pattern of this cloth is supposed to resemble clouds in the sky at sunset, hence its name 'cloud brocade'. Production of cloud brocade started in the Six Dynasties (186-580). It is ornate, heavy and regal: as such it was extensively used by imperial households. During the reign of the Kangxi Emperor (1661-1723) there were 30,000 looms and 50,000 workers producing brocade in Nanjing for export to Europe and Japan as well as for use by the court and mandarinate. The premier grade is stiff and very ornate and is only used for wall hangings; the second grade (which today is widely exported) for lavish garments.

The largest Nanjing factory is now semi-automated. As you enter its dark hangar-like workshop the noise of the hundred or so machines is deafening — the workers wear no ear-mufflers. Each girl is responsible for about five machines. She moves from one to another, checking the tension, rethreading the spool and correcting any error in pattern, her source of light a solitary bulb hanging over the loom. In one of the smaller factories, it is possible to see the vast wooden looms of yesterday at work. Each one is operated by two people: the craftsman in front of the spindles and shuttle, with his assistant high up on a platform operating the thread lines that control the pattern.

Excursion to Yangzhou

The ancient city of Yangzhou is renowned for its cuisine, beautiful women, arts and scholarship: a visit is strongly recommended. It is north of the Yangzi, 1½ hours' coach ride from Nanjing. In the Tang Dynasty (618-907) we know Yangzhou was a thriving city of 80,000 people. From the 14th to the 18th centuries most of its wealth came from salt, which was transported north and south along the Grand Canal which forms the eastern boundary of the city. But in the late 19th century, with changes in the salt administration, its fortunes changed. Then when the railways came to China, it was decided to ferry the trains across the turbulent Yangzi further upstream at Nanjing. Today Yangzhou offers the visitor a wealth of things to look at and enjoy. For the tourist who wishes to stay longer there is the excellent Xiyuan Hotel. Also a new eight-story hotel is under construction.

Food

Yangzhou food is one of the famous cuisines of China: less bland than Cantonese, less spicy than Sichuanese, and less heavy than Pekingese. Yangzhou is also famous for its knives and many of the dishes are delicately sliced: cold beancurd cut into long slender strips dressed with sesame oil and decorated with cucumber and chili, for example. Other specialities include 'lion's head' casserole with freshwater crab, and 'drunken' prawns — small uncooked prawns marinated in local wine.

Shopping

Handicrafts Six original crafts of Yangzhou are still practised: lacquer and stone ware, jade, ivory and bamboo carving, and papercuts. One can visit factories engaged in all of these and buy the finished articles. The ancient processes and designs are being revived as well as new ones introduced: standards are high.

Bonsai Yangzhou has several famous bonsai nurseries. Buy some by all means, but be prepared for transportation problems.

Sights of Yangzhou

Slender West Lake

This is a beautiful man-made lake (named 'Shouxi' in

Chinese) dating from the Tang Dynasty. It is surrounded by
Qing Dynasty pavilions with poetic names such as the Pavilion
to Hear the Birds Singing. Across the middle of the lake is the
Five Pavilion Bridge, its yellow roofs perched on a triple-
arched grey stone bridge. A copy of the Qianlong Emperor's
pleasure boat now sails visitors round the lake. During a visit
the Qianlong Emperor was enjoying the beauties of the lake:
he commented to one of the salt merchants how pleasant it
would be to see a dagoba nearby. So in awe of the emperor
were they that, during the night, they carved a full-sized
dagoba from salt. The emperor was duly impressed and, when
he returned north, the permanent version which stands today
near the bridge was built.

Yangzhou Museum
Given its historical connection with the arts it is no surprise
to discover a good museum in Yangzhou. In the 1780s a
group of painters, later known as the Eight Eccentrics,
disillusioned with the unimaginative trends of contemporary
painting, formed the Yangzhou School. They developed their
own style and, as their fame spread, many artists gathered in
Yangzhou to study under them. Their work is well represented
in the museum as are the crafts of Yangzhou, including
interesting examples of a now dead craft — brick carving. In
the garden of the museum is a well-preserved tomb of a Han
Dynasty man and wife, and a 15-yard long Tang canoe which
would have been carried on a sailing ship as a landing craft.

Qianlong Boathouse and Pier
There is a charming pier and boathouse where the
Qianlong Emperor used to alight when visiting his Yangzhou
palace. He is reported to have eaten in the restaurant where
today one can have a delicious Chinese breakfast of
dumplings, noodles and sesame seed buns.

Flat Hill
This spot to the northwest of the city centre has several
interesting sights to which visitors are taken.
Flat Hill Residence On the western edge of the group
of buildings on Flat Hill, there is Flat Hill Residence, the house
of a famous Northern Song scholar and essayist, Ouyang Xiu.
The renowned Song poet Su Dongpo is believed to have lived
there also.
Daming Temple This was constructed in the Song
Dynasty. The Qianlong Emperor changed the temple name to

Fajing, but the original name persisted and, in recent years, has again become widely adopted. The main hall of the temple, Daxiong, dates from the Tang and is a serene building in front of which rise up the twisted barks of eight whispering pines. In the courtyard of this building grows the rare and renowned flower Qionghua (Hortensia). It is said that, so intoxicated by its beauty and fragrance was the emperor Sui Yang Di that he had the Grand Canal built in order to get to Yangzhou quickly. In 616, when the rebellions in the north became too much for him, he retreated down the canal to Yangzhou.

Jian Zhen Memorial Hall Jian Zhen was an eighth-century monk who travelled widely to spread the teachings of Buddhism, reaching Japan on his sixth expedition. In 1963 eminent Buddhists and scholars in China and Japan decided to erect a hall to Jian Zhen's memory. The Song-style monastery (completed in 1973) is today inhabited by several monks.

The Fifth Spring under Heaven Proceeding westwards from the group of buildings into the Western Garden, you will come upon one of the seven famed springs of China. In the Tang Dynasty these springs were graded according to their compatibility with tea. This one on Flat Hill was ranked fifth.

Suzhou fan factory

Suzhou

Introduction

Suzhou, situated on the Grand Canal 42 miles to the northwest of Shanghai, is a fascinating ancient city of some 630,000 people. It was founded around 600BC under King Helü of the Kingdom of Wu. The building of the Grand Canal in 605 opened up an important trade route to the north for Suzhou's already thriving silk industry. By the time of Marco Polo's visit in about 1276 Suzhou was the size it is today, as one can see from a 12th-century map now in the Temple of Confucius. He would have found the city surrounded by a moated wall (just recently demolished) and six gates (of which two remain). 'Let me tell you' he enthused, 'in this city there are fully 6000 stone bridges'. Today, however, there are just 300. Marco Polo also noted Suzhou's 'capable merchants and skilled practitioners of every craft and among them wise philosophers'. These wise philosophers were principally responsible for creating Suzhou's exquisite gardens. 500 years after Marco Polo's visit Sir George Staunton, chronicler of Lord MacCartney's Embassy to China in 1973, recorded: 'the gentlemen of the embassy also thought that the women of Sou-choo handsomer, fairer and dressed in better taste'. So with flourishing trade, beautiful women, the literati and their stylish gardens, it was indeed the case that 'in heaven there is paradise, on earth Suzhou and Hangzhou'.

Present-day Suzhou gives the impression of having changed little. It is still a city of narrow streets. Large bamboo poles laden with airing bedclothes hang from low whitewashed houses. Plane trees throw a dappled light on passers-by. Stone bridges cross the numerous busy canals. People converse in the charming, slightly coy dialect (it is even said to be pleasant listening to an argument in Suzhou). The city has retained and is proud of its garden heritage (11 large, 34 medium and 69 small ones remain). Certainly the women are still strikingly beautiful although this aspect cannot be reduced to precise statistics. While the volume of trade has been eclipsed by the Shanghai metropolis, Suzhou still thrives economically. It has maintained its world reputation for traditional handicrafts, particularly embroidery. In the Qing Dynasty a large percentage of the successful candidates in the civil service examinations came from Suzhou, and today the city continues to be a centre of learning.

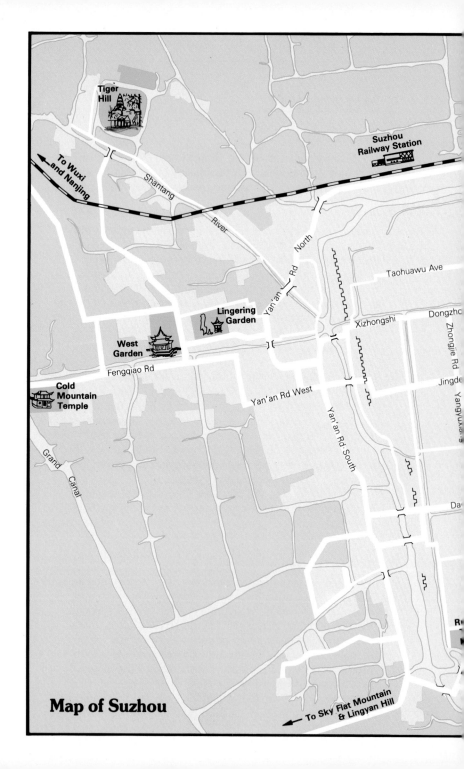

Map of Suzhou

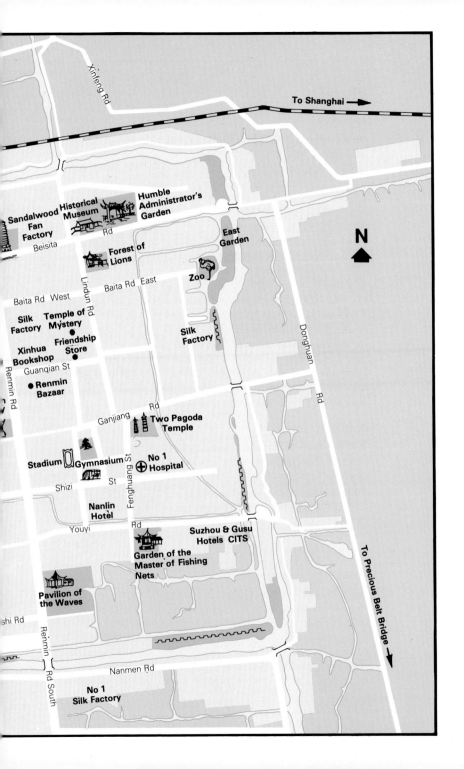

To Shanghai →

Xinfeng Rd

Sandalwood Fan Factory

Historical Museum

Humble Administrator's Garden

Rd

Beisita

East Garden

Forest of Lions

Zoo

Baita Rd West

Lindun Rd

Baita Rd East

Silk Factory

Temple of Mystery

Xinhua Bookshop

Friendship Store

Silk Factory

Donghuan Rd

Guanqian St

Renmin Rd

Renmin Bazaar

Ganjiang

Rd

Two Pagoda Temple

Stadium

Gymnasium

Fenghuang St

No 1 Hospital

Shizi

St

Nanlin Hotel

Youyi

Rd

Suzhou & Gusu Hotels CITS

Garden of the Master of Fishing Nets

Pavilion of the Waves

shi Rd

Renmin Rd South

Nanmen Rd

No 1 Silk Factory

To Precious Belt Bridge →

N

Hotels

苏州饭店 友谊路115号
SUZHOU HOTEL 115 Youyi Road tel. 4646
This hotel, in the heart of the old city, is set in a pleasing
garden and consists of two buildings. The old one has 56
rooms, all of them spacious and with private bathrooms. The
nine-storey new building has 140 smaller but quite comfortable
rooms with private bathrooms. There is a restaurant in both
buildings but the post office, clinic, barber, and arts and crafts
shop are in the new one. Also sharing these facilities is the new
Gusu Hotel, which is hidden behind a large yew hedge.

古苏饭店 友谊路115号
GUSU HOTEL 115 Youyi Road tel. 4646
This new hotel has 110 rooms. It was built by the same
concern as the one that put up the Dingshan Guesthouse
extension in Nanjing and Shuixiu Hotel in Wuxi (to which it is
identical both in lay-out and decor — mimosa pattern
wallpaper and squeaky acrylic carpet). In addition to the
facilities shared with Suzhou Hotel, the Gusu has a restaurant
and an arts and crafts shop.

南林饭店 滚绣坊19号
NANLIN HOTEL 19 Gunxiu Fang tel. 4441
Also off the charming Youyi Road, this old hotel is a complex
of six buildings. It has 160 rooms in all — large, old-fashioned
and all with good-sized bathrooms. There is a restaurant, arts
and crafts shop, clinic, bank and post office. If you are staying
in one of the outlying buildings, you may order your food in
your room which will be brought from the kitchen in ravishing
lacquer baskets.

南园宾馆 友谊路251号
NANYUAN GUESTHOUSE 251 Youyi Road tel. 4641
Across the street from Nanlin Hotel is this guesthouse. It is
usually reserved for government guests but, if it is not
occupied, small groups will be housed here: there are 10
rooms. The bedrooms and sitting room are very spacious and
well decorated in traditional Chinese style with beautiful scroll
paintings. The food is excellent.

Restaurants

The daily menus for tourists in the three hotels are good.
The hotel cooks use an imaginative variety of fish and
vegetables. The *dianxin* at Nanlin Hotel is excellent. Four-
happiness steamed dumplings — succulent shrimp and green
pepper filled morsels — are particularly good.

松鹤楼 观前街141号
SONGHELOU 141 Guanqian Street tel. 2066
This is an old restaurant where, reputedly, the Qianlong
Emperor (1736-96) ate. Until recently it had only 40 tables
and was in an old building, its ovens outside in the open air. It
has now been rehoused in a three-storey modern block and
has 120 tables. The food is good though with a slight greasy
tendency. Songhelou, or the Pine and Crane Restaurant, is
known for its delicate chopping so try the finely-sliced eel with
mushrooms, sweet ham and fresh bamboo shoot. A famous
delicacy is a soup of fish and tiny lotus leaves covered in their
lake slime. A local Qing Dynasty official is supposed to have so
yearned for these that he gave up his official post in Peking.

涵碧楼 东园
HANBILOU Dongyuan tel. 2722
This is a recently-opened restaurant in the new East Garden.
The head chef and teacher is an old man who, incredible
though it may seem, cooked for one of the noble households
at the end of the Qing Dynasty.

苏州菜馆 观前街
SUZHOU RESTAURANT Guanqian Street tel. 2392
This restaurant has a good general menu serving several
vegetarian dishes. Their 'squirrel' fish or the 'peony' turtle are
also worth trying.

黄天源糕团店 观前街88号
HUANGTIANYUAN CAKE SHOP 88 Guanqian Street
tel. 5896
Suzhou is famous for its sweets and cakes. This shop was
opened in 1838, although Huangtianyuan has been in
business for 200 years. It is reputed to make 160 different

kinds of cakes and pastries, the repertoire changing with the
seasons. The main ingredient for many of these is glutinous
rice, but red bean, egg yolk, cocoa, green bean, sesame,
preserved fruits, pumpkinseed, walnut and almond are all used
in countless permutations to give a variety of taste, colour
and texture. You can either eat at the shop (with chopsticks),
or order a selection by telephone.

新聚丰　人民路657号
XINJUFENG RESTAURANT 657 Renmin Road tel. 3794
This is a good place to try the local cuisine, particularly the
dishes consisting of crab, shrimp or eel.

Shopping

The pleasures of Suzhou shopping are manifold: not only
is there a multitude of good things to buy, but wandering
between the various shops — conveniently grouped together
in narrow Guanqian Street — provides a close-at-hand
encounter with the daily life of Suzhou. Old men pore over
chess sets; women, baskets laden, hurry home, while others
linger to chat; grandpas push their charges in bamboo
perambulators; bright-eyed little girls skip and play cat's cradle
with elastic bands.

Visit the Friendship Store: it has a good antique
department on the top floor. Then cross Guanqian Street to
the fabric shop Qiantaixiang which is filled with bales of smart
striped cottons (59 *fen* per yard in 1980) as well as silks,
synthetics, velours and so on. Customers' change whizzes
overhead in 'mini space craft'. Next door is a pen and paper
shop. The Chinese (like the Florentines) are stationery addicts
and these shops are always a joy — watercoloured greetings
cards, papercuts, and book-markers decorated with elegant
Qing ladies. Two away is Caizhizhai, the candy store. Suzhou
is famous for sweets, such as preserved strawberries rolled in
white sugar, and this attractive old shop displays its wares both
in large jars and in rows of waist-high wooden boxes with glass
lids which form the counter. They do a roaring trade in the
bonbons it is customary to give guests at Chinese weddings.

Walking the other way down Guanqian Street countless
interesting shops unfurl. Immediately behind the Friendship
Store is a square dominated by a Qing Daoist temple (the
Temple of Mystery), in front of which are rows of tailors
hunched over sewing machines. This is also the place to come

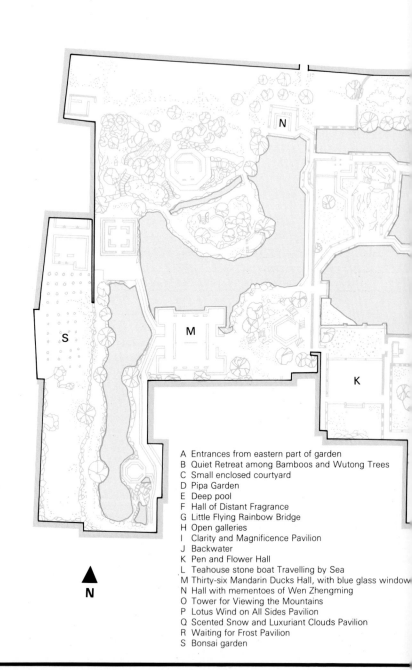

A Entrances from eastern part of garden
B Quiet Retreat among Bamboos and Wutong Trees
C Small enclosed courtyard
D Pipa Garden
E Deep pool
F Hall of Distant Fragrance
G Little Flying Rainbow Bridge
H Open galleries
I Clarity and Magnificence Pavilion
J Backwater
K Pen and Flower Hall
L Teahouse stone boat Travelling by Sea
M Thirty-six Mandarin Ducks Hall, with blue glass window
N Hall with mementoes of Wen Zhengming
O Tower for Viewing the Mountains
P Lotus Wind on All Sides Pavilion
Q Scented Snow and Luxuriant Clouds Pavilion
R Waiting for Frost Pavilion
S Bonsai garden

N

Map of the Main Section of the Humble Administrator's Garden

Map © Maggie Keswick

if you want to buy vegetables, nails or lambswool coatlinings. There is another antique shop away from here on Renmin Road which is well worth a visit.

Gardens of Suzhou

Garden of the Master of Fishing Nets

One discovers this, the most exciting and indeed the smallest garden (just one acre) in Suzhou down an alleyway in the centre of the city. You enter through a nondescript door which gives no hint of what lies beyond. A sharp right turn takes you into the first courtyard — this not only helps divorce the garden from its urban surroundings but prevents demons (who cannot make sharp turns) from entering. Here you feel compelled to walk on: one of the many subtleties of Chinese gardens is that the visitor is only shown a little at a time, so he constantly anticipates more secrets round the corner. The pathway leads the visitor in and out of pavilions and courtyards around the lake — which mirrors them to perfection — over the smallest bridge in Suzhou to the residence.

The garden, originally called Fisherman's Retreat, was built in 1140 by a government official named Shi Zhengzhi. Over the next 600 years it changed hands many times and fell into disrepair until, in 1770, Song Zongyuan, also a government official, restored it. He gave it its present name, Wangshiyuan. One of the buildings in the garden, the Hall for Staying Spring, and its courtyard have been copied and are now on show in New York's Metropolitan Museum.

Humble Administrator's Garden

In the early Ming Dynasty a politician named Wang Xianchen created this garden with the help of his painter friend, Wen Zhengming (the collaboration of an artist gave a garden celebrity). The name Zhuozhengyuan can be translated many ways, 'Unsuccessful Politician's Garden' giving the best clue to its origin. It took 16 years to complete and was later gambled away by the owner's son to the owner of Liu Garden.

The garden is in two parts. The eastern section is a large institutionalised park, at the far end of which is a wall. Passing through this you enter the garden proper. This is broken into a series of islands and pathways zigzagging across the lake — there is as much water as land. This plan allows the visitor a good view of the pavilions (such as the Thirty-six Mandarin Ducks Pavilion) he will eventually visit. Towards the end of the garden is the small intimate Pipa (Loquat) Garden: its paved courtyards provide fine examples of pebble pictures.

Lingering Garden

The Lingering Garden, or Liu Garden, was laid out in 1525 by a civil servant named Xu Shitai. He called it the East Garden to distinguish it from the West Garden which he also created. Acquired later by Liu Rongfeng, it became known as Liu's Garden. Since then, its name has undergone another change — the present name, though sounding the same as the earlier owner's surname, is another character meaning 'to remain'.

At 10 acres it is the largest Suzhou garden and is in three parts. The visitor is led clockwise through the vast rockeries (which back onto the lake) of the western and northern sections. Following the winding path the visitor emerges to find the lake spread out before him, its surface broken by a zigzag bridge clad in wisteria. He then moves into the more formal halls and courtyards of the eastern section.

An intriguing feature of this garden are its fanciful windows. These *huo chuang* ('windows which are alive') are all shapes and sizes, some with lattice work. They focus the visitor's eye, zoom lens-like, on a rock collection with bamboo, the mirror image of a rock, a *trompe l'oeil* picture above a formal setting of a table and two chairs, or just another visitor posing to have a picture taken. Towards the end of the garden opposite the Hall of Mandarin Ducks is the largest and most prestigious Tai Lake rock (see page 82) in Suzhou.

Pavilion of the Waves

Pavilion of the Waves (or Canglangting), the oldest garden in Suzhou, was laid out in 1044 on the site of a 10th-century house. Its name, coined by the Song poet Su Zimei, derives (somewhat obscurely) from a much earlier traditional poem: 'If the water of the Canglang river is clean, I wash the ribbons of my official hat in it; if it is dirty, I wash my feet.' 'Canglang' broadly translates as wave or tide, and was widely used by Song writers as an image for the ups and downs of life.

The garden's layout is original; the pavilions, however, have been destroyed and rebuilt many times, most recently in

1927. It was not until 1954 that Canglangting was once more open to the public. One third of the area is taken up by a false mountain, with the Canglangting itself (*ting* means pavilion) standing on the top. The garden is also renowned for the calligraphy — to be found on the steles and pillars of its pavilions — including a particularly fine example of the Qianlong Emperor's hand. The names of pavilions and other key spots provide one of the many pleasures of Chinese gardens, and the Canglangting has some splendid ones such as the Hall Where One Smells Marvellous Perfumes, and Pavilion Requiring the Utmost Respect and Admiration. The garden also provides an excellent example of the concept of 'borrowed landscape'. The designer omitted to build a perimeter wall and was therefore able to 'borrow' the adjacent canal into the garden. This creates the illusion of extended space and leaves the visitor bewildered as to where the garden ends.

Main Hall of West Garden Temple, Suzhou

Forest of Lions

The garden most famous for its rock formations is the Shizilin — Forest of Lions. It was commissioned by a monk, Tian Ru, in memory of his teacher Zhong Feng; the character sound for 'teacher' or 'master' and 'lion' are homophones, hence 'Forest of Lions'. Sometimes the garden's name is attributed to the shape of its rocks, which resemble lions.

This rock lovers' paradise was laid out in 1350 with the help of Ni Yuanzhen, one of the 'Four Great Masters' of the Yuan Dynasty. As already mentioned, to have a famous artist associated with a garden gave it cachet and lasting fame. Indeed 'men of impeccable qualities would not sit about in inferior gardens'. The family of the renowned American Chinese architect I.M. Pei were Shizilin's last owners.

On his tour of the garden the visitor is led in and out of the labyrinth of Tai Lake rocks which couple the pavilions surrounding an artificial lake. Overlooking a marble boat is the Pavilion of Gentle Perfume and Spreading Shade. On the top floor of this charming building is a tea-room cum antique shop. Nearby is the delightfully named Kiosk Where One Questions the Plum Tree.

Garden of Joy

The Garden of Joy or, in Chinese, Yiyuan, was laid out around 1875 by Gu Wenbin, a rich government official, at the cost of 200,000 ounces of silver. Ideas from the earlier gardens were skilfully employed and indeed Tai Lake rocks discarded from other sites were used. It is a small — just over an acre — intricate and delightful garden.

All the gardens mentioned are popular and therefore very crowded. They open at 7.30am so why not visit them early, enjoy the peace and tranquillity they deserve and return to your hotel for a hearty Chinese breakfast?

Other Sights of Suzhou

West Garden Temple

In the Ming Dynasty a mandarin named Xu Shitai created two gardens to the northwest of the city. One, West Garden, was given by his son to a Buddhist community which had a temple built there. During the Taiping Rebellion the temple was unfortunately sacked and burnt, so the present structure dates from 1892. Today visitors enter through majestic yellow gates leading to a large courtyard surrounded by buildings. The Buddha in the main hall is guarded on the right by the Hall of Four Celestial Guards, and on the left by the Hall of 500 Arhats (disciples of the Buddha). Behind the Buddha is a vast Goddess of Mercy. Walk through this complex and you will discover the Life Sparing Pond where lurks a Ming Dynasty turtle. (This would put his or her age at no less than 336. There are apparently documents to support this seemingly incredible phenomenon. The turtle of course is a symbol of longevity.) Each summer before the rains this animal, as big as a table-top, comes to the surface.

Precious Belt Bridge

Four miles southeast of Suzhou, where the Grand Canal and Yantai Lake meet, is a simple, low, stone bridge of 53 arches dating from the Tang Dynasty (618-907). Its name derives from an act of generosity by the governor of the day who, to help defray building costs, contributed his precious jade belt. Sadly a modern bridge has been built within 10 feet and a row of telephone poles placed on top of the old bridge. Its ample arches provide local fishermen with a sheltered spot to prepare food and rest from the hurly-burly of the Grand Canal.

Historical Museum

The Historical Museum in Beisita Road is housed in the residential building of the Humble Administrator's Garden. There is an interesting collection of exhibits, especially Song Dynasty silk clothes, samplers and others domestic knick-knacks.

Northern Pagoda

A nine-story wooden pagoda stands to the west of the Historical Museum. A pagoda was first built on this site by Sun Quan, the founder of the State of Wu (229-280) — not to be confused with the much earlier Kingdom of Wu which is associated with the founding of Suzhou in 600BC. Today's pagoda dates from the Southern Song (1127-1279) and was extensively restored under the Kangxi Emperor (1661-1723). Repairs are now again underway, so the pagoda will soon be open to tourists.

Cold Mountain Temple

Situated to the west of the city this Qing temple (the original Liang temple was burnt) is today inhabited by five monks. It is named Hanshan, or Cold Mountain, after the place to which one of its founding residents retired. In front of

the fine yellow entrance a graceful high-arched Tang bridge crosses the busy canal. In former times heavily laden barges would have stopped off to sell their wares at the thriving market the monks ran (scarcely in accordance with the teachings of their faith but apparently with impunity). Inside the small compound, to the right of the main hall, is a bell tower: the present bell (replaced by the Japanese) dates from 1901 as the original Tang one was carried off to Japan and then lost.

The sound of the Tang bell is said to have travelled far, and has been immortalized in a contemporary poem by Zhang Ji: 'The moon goes down, the crow cries, cold fills the air; under the Feng (Maple) Bridge, the lantern lights prevent sleep; beyond Suzhou is the Hanshansi; through the night, the sound of its bells comes as far as my boat.'

Beside the bell tower is a stele pavilion, housing many inscriptions, Zhang Ji's poem included, and a poignant poem written by Kang Youwei after the cherished bell was removed by the Japanese: 'The sound of the bell has crossed the sea to the east; a cold silence invades the Hanshansi.'

Tiger Hill, Suzhou

Tiger Hill

In 473BC King Helü of the Kingdom of Wu was struck a mortal blow by King Goujian of the Kingdom of Yue. His body was returned to Suzhou, his capital, and buried here (although his tomb has never been found). The third day afterwards a white tiger is said to have appeared to guard the tomb, hence the name Tiger Hill.

This picturesque hill, northwest of the city, is alive with stories from the Wu and Yue Kingdoms (Spring and Autumn period). Ascending the hill you pass the Sword Testing Rock which the King of Wu reputedly split when trying his sword, the Pillow Stone where a famous monk rested, a Liang Dynasty well and then the Thousand Men Stone from which after rain blood reputedly flows. This legend originates from the execution of 1000 workers in order to keep secret the whereabouts of Helü's tomb. Still higher is the Pond of Swords, the traditional burial place of Helü and his 3000 swords. Finally at the summit is the leaning octagonal 150-foot pagoda. The original six storeys date from 961; the seventh is not original but was rebuilt in the 17th century. It is now considerably reinforced to prevent disaster. The nearby temple was burnt seven times, the present structure dating from after the Taiping Rebellion.

Sky Flat Mountain

Twelve miles southwest of the city is this striking maple tree-clad hill. Many of the trees at the foot of the mountain were planted in the Ming Dynasty and are some 400 years old. On the hillside remain several pavilions: the most well known are Gaoyiyuan or, by another name, Letianlou, built in the Qianlong period (1736-96) to commemorate the Tang poet Bai Juyi; and the Royal Stele Pavilion, also built in the Qing Dynasty, to display a stone tablet on which was engraved a poem about a visit to the Sky Flat Mountain by Emperor Qianlong. Other notable sights are strange grotesque rock formations and an interesting narrow gorge known as A Glimpse of Sky.

Lingyan Hill

Further to the west of Sky Flat Mountain, 30 miles from Suzhou, is Lingyan Hill. This too is the source of many legends from the Wu and Yue Kingdoms (sixth century BC). The King of Wu built a palace here for Xi Shi, his favourite beauty (who it transpired was a spy planted by the Kingdom of Yue). From Lingyan Temple, which stands on the top of the hill, you can obtain a superb view of the surroundings including Tai Lake.

Factories

Silk 'They live by trade and industry, have silk in great quantity and make silken cloth for their clothing': thus wrote Marco Polo. Indeed Suzhou has for centuries been famous for its silk which was probably its most important industry by the time of his visit in the 13th century.

Today there are three silk factories in Suzhou, two weaving mills and the Embroidery Research Institute. Visitors are usually taken to see the Embroidery Research Institute, which was opened in 1957 to preserve traditional methods and to research new ones. It specializes in three types of embroidery — single- and double-face work, Kossu and modern cross-stitch.

Most famous are the double-faced pictures of fluffy white Shandong cats with one blue and one brown eye, or of cassia or gold fish. These embroideries are worked with silk thread on nylon fabric. The skilled embroiderer splits the silk into 48 barely visible strands. The incredibly delicate finished article is specially framed so that it can be viewed from both sides. The latest idea is to produce a double-side portrait of a lady.

Kossu is a type of brocade, again double-faced, which dates from the Song Dynasty (960-1280). Woven into the cloth are tiny gaps, like the holes in lace but far fewer. The finished piece is framed and then placed so it can be seen from both sides. The pinpricks of light shinning through the little holes create a remarkable effect. Kossu is woven by hand on large old wooden looms. It can take a craftsman a year to finish a copy of a large Song or Tang piece.

Lastly the modern stitch, which is used to produce copies of western old masters such as the Mona Lisa, or famous Chinese sights such as the Yangzi River Bridge.

There is a shop at the Institute, but most of the major pieces are sent on exhibition overseas, are used to decorate new hotels or are given to important state guests.

Fans The craft of making fans is probably 2000 years old. There are two types of traditional fan, folding and fixed (made either of silk or paper on a bamboo frame, or of carved ivory). During the past 100 years carved sandalwood fans have also become popular. Throughout imperial days both men and women carried fans not only as cooling aids but also for gesticulation. Fashion dictated mens' fans to be of nine to 24 pleats, whereas ladies' were to be of no fewer than 30.

The present Suzhou Sandalwood Fan Factory is housed in a beautiful Ming building which, during the Taiping Heavenly Kingdom, was the king's residence. Today there is a workforce of 180 producing over 200,000 full sized and two million small fans per annum. There is a well-stocked shop where visitors are taken after seeing round the factory.

Excursion to Changshu

A little over an hour by road (less by rail) from Suzhou is Changshu. This is a fascinating town with 3000 years of history. There are several fine monuments, including a well-preserved square Ming pagoda, the top storeys of which are made from 30,000 catties of bronze (a catty is approximately 1¼ pounds). Changshu's pride is its traditional lace-making in which 15,000 of its 100,000 inhabitants are engaged. It is largely conducted as a cottage industry but visitors may visit the factory (which holds a national production prize) where exquisite table linen and bedcovers are produced.

Changshu's name which means 'always ripe' refers to the very productive farmland surrounding the town. Apart from the normal crops — rice and wheat — of the region, Changshu's agricultural produce includes cassia, chestnuts (the trees are underplanted with tea), red beans (a symbol of love), and a special type of glutinous rice. (In addition, cultured pearls and mink are also farmed.) All this, together with the fact that the area is famous for game and fish, contribute to the excellence of its food. Try cassia flower and chestnut soup (sweet and delicious), a rare pond carp (held in high esteem by the Qianlong Emperor) and Beggar's Chicken, a widely-renowned dish in Chinese cuisine which is said by some to have originated in Changshu.

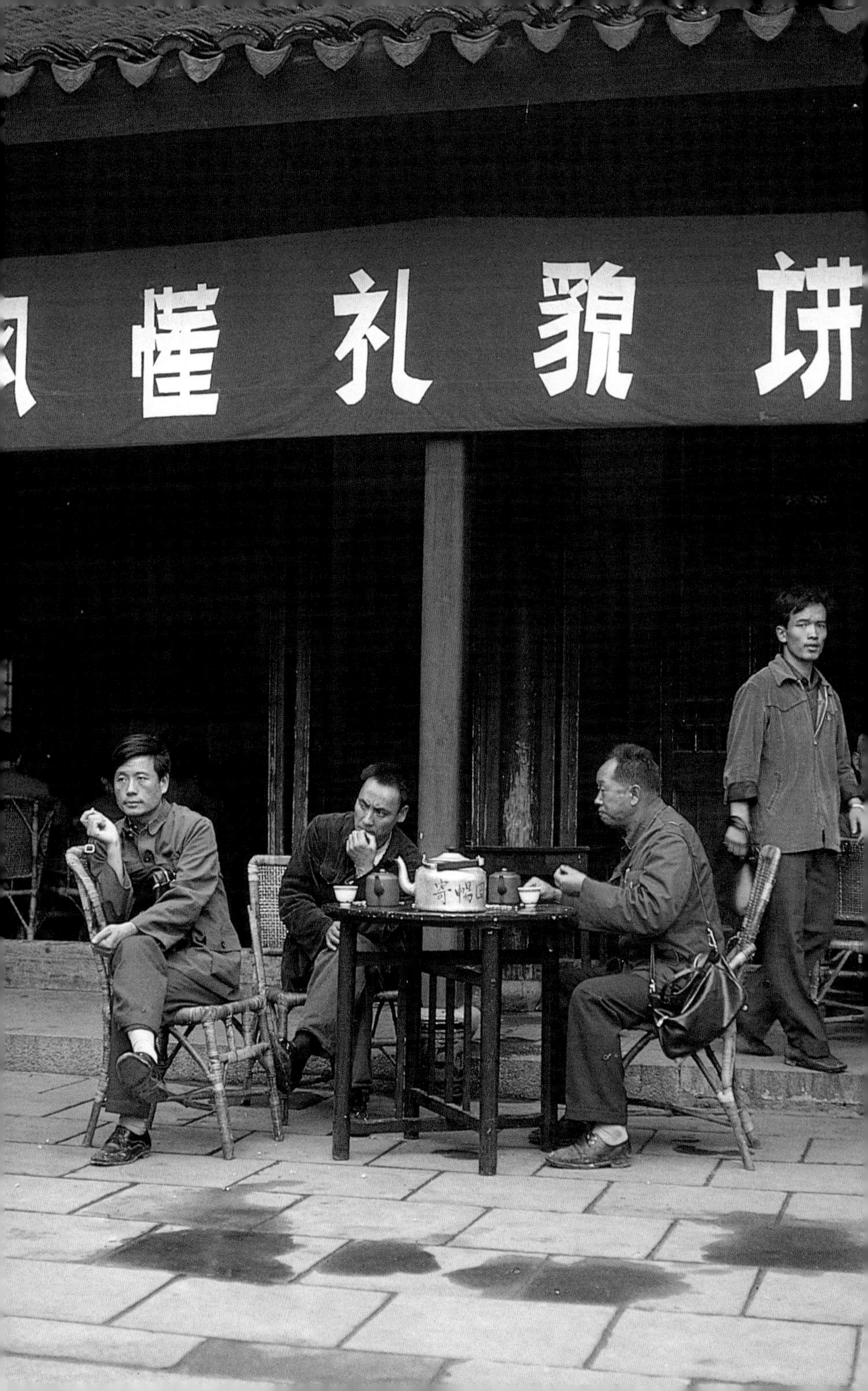
懂 礼 貌

Wuxi

Introduction

Wuxi, according to tradition, was originally founded some 3000 years ago by Tai Bo, the eldest son of Prince Tai of the Zhou Dynasty (1122-770BC). He established the State of Wu with its capital at Mei just to the east of the present city centre: his tomb is there to this day. Legend has it that, as a result of tin being discovered around 206BC, Mei was renamed Youxi — 'with tin' — but come 25AD the deposits ran out and it was given its present name Wuxi — 'without tin'. For the next 1900 years Wuxi remained a quiet and rather poor market town. But in the 1930s, attracted by its strategic communications — the Grand Canal and the Shanghai/ Peking railway — a group of businessmen chose to inject large sums into Wuxi industry and the population grew to 500,000.

Since 1949, both Wuxi's industry and its agriculture have expanded. Today its population totals 750,000 of which its 407 factories employ 180,000; the agricultural community produces three harvests per annum — two of rice and one of wheat — generating a ton of food per acre.

By contrast, wander along a narrow cobbled street and pause on an arched stone bridge over a canal — part of the network which interlaces the city. Watch the groups of women chat while washing vegetables and clothes on the steps of the whitewashed houses, or follow the progress of a line of lighters, powered by pole, snaking its way from one bridge to the next. And ponder how the Grand Canal, built almost fourteen centuries ago, is still a focal point of the economy and society of Wuxi.

Hotels

太湖饭店　锡梅路

TAI LAKE HOTEL Ximei Road tel. 2398
This hotel, some four miles from the city centre, has fine views over Tai Lake and the surrounding farmland. It was built as a school prior to 1949 and subsequently converted. The 120 rooms are old-fashioned but pleasant, each with a private bath. There is a post office, a shop and a good restaurant.

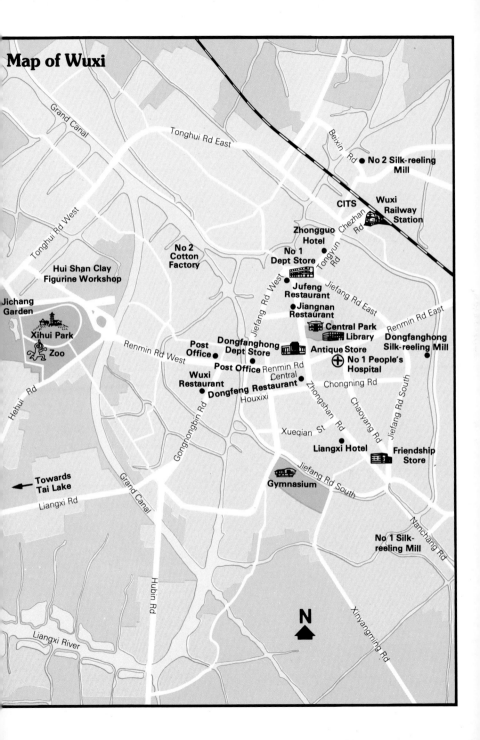

Map of Wuxi

Grand Canal

Tonghui Rd East

Beixin Rd

● No 2 Silk-reeling Mill

Tonghui Rd West

CITS

Chezhan Rd

Wuxi Railway Station

Zhongguo Hotel

No 2 Cotton Factory

No 1 Dept Store

Tongyun Rd

Jiefang Rd East

Hui Shan Clay Figurine Workshop

Jiefang Rd West

Jufeng Restaurant

● Jiangnan Restaurant

Renmin Rd East

Jichang Garden

Central Park

Library

Dongfanghong Silk-reeling Mill

Xihui Park

Zoo

Renmin Rd West

Post Office

Dongfanghong Dept Store

Antique Store

⊕ No 1 People's Hospital

Hehui Rd

Post Office

Renmin Rd Central

Chongning Rd

Jiefang Rd South

Wuxi Restaurant

Dongfeng Restaurant

Houxixi

Zhongshan Rd

Chaoyang Rd

Gonghongbin Rd

Xueqian St

Towards Tai Lake

Liangxi Hotel

Friendship Store

Grand Canal

Liangxi Rd

Jiefang Rd South

Gymnasium

No 1 Silk-reeling Mill

Nanchang Rd

Hubin Rd

N

Liangxi River

Xinyangming Rd

湖滨饭店 蠡园路
HUBIN HOTEL Liyuan Road tel. 5824
Hubin Hotel is ideally situated on the shores of Li Lake, overlooking the lake and the attractive Li Garden. The eight-storey hotel, opened in 1978, has 350 bedrooms with private bath, and houses a number of facilities which it shares with the nearby Shuixiu Hotel. These include a barber's shop, a clinic, a bank which will issue foreign currency certificates against credit cards, masseurs who will come to your room, two large shops, a post office, a coffee shop and a restaurant.

水秀饭店 蠡园路
SHUIXIU HOTEL Liyuan Road tel. 2985
The Shuixiu is a two-storey motel style prefabricated structure, standing beside Hubin Hotel and with equally splendid views across Li Lake. Built in 1980, it is identical to the low budget hotels put up in Suzhou and Nanjing by the same company. The 110 rooms and bathrooms are tiny, but all have airconditioning and colour television. The walls are paper thin, so try and avoid snoring neighbours. The hotel has its own dining room but the rest of the facilities are next door except for the Shuixiu's pièce de résistance — a disco. For a small entry fee you can dance from 7.30pm-11.30pm.

中国饭店 通运路81号
ZHONGGUO HOTEL 81 Tongyun Road tel. 3438
This is the only hotel in the centre of town. It is at present reserved for Chinese visitors and has 500 beds.

Restaurants

The 12,000 tons of fish (of some 30 varieties) landed at Wuxi every year understandably provide its culinary emphasis. The tiny silver fish (similar to whitebait) are Wuxi's most famous. From its non-fish speciality, spare ribs, Wuxi gained the title 'Little Shanghai'. This alludes to the innate merchant cunning involved in turning bones with little meat into a delicacy (and also in using the clay from Hui Shan to produce money-making statues).

江南菜馆 中山路435号
JIANGNAN 435 Zhongshan Road tel. 3651
The Jiangnan is excellent, extremely good value and recently opened to foreign visitors. For 6.50 *yuan* per head you can

have a delicious nine-course dinner. Dew Drop Duck is a must.
First the duck is soaked in pink salt water (hence the skin
colour), then marinated and cooked in local wine: the result is
tender and succulent.

无锡馄饨馆 中山路391号
WUXI HUNTUN RESTAURANT 391 Zhongshan Road
tel. 2484
Wuxi Huntun Restaurant is an old restaurant near the railway
station. It is a bustling, popular place serving good *dianxin* —
both savoury and sweet snacks including *huntun* (small
dumplings served fried or in soup).

Shopping

Wuxi is not a shoppers' paradise to compare with either
Nanjing or Suzhou, but there is still plenty to look at. After the
hotels, all of which have well-stocked shops, the centre of
town is the best place to browse. At 192 Renmin Road is a
large Arts and Crafts Store. Just to the south of Dongfanghong
Square at 466 Zhongshan Road, you will find the antique

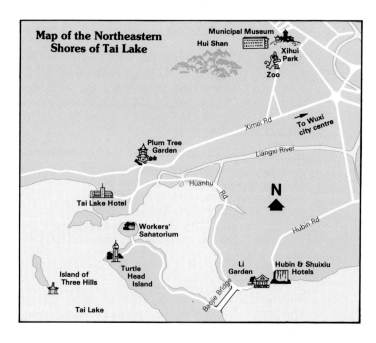

Wuxi street scene

shop and, on your way back to the square, there is Dongfanghong Department Store. On weekdays the shops close at 7pm but on Saturdays they stay open late, and food and knick-knack stalls are set up outside creating a night market.

Sights of Wuxi
Tai Lake

Some four miles from Wuxi is the vast Tai Lake which at almost 1400 square miles is China's fourth largest. More than 90 islands are spread over the lake's surface. Along its northern shores there is a hive of agricultural activity — geese and duck farms; fish farms where to gain space the fish are housed, with exquisite Chinese ingenuity, in seven layers according to species; peach and plum orchards; and acres of mulberry trees for the silk worms. Parts of the lake have been divided by causeways to make lotus and water-chestnut beds. The area is a favourite with the Chinese: the shores are scattered with retreats for government officials, and packed cruise boats take day-trippers from Shanghai round the lake.

There are four flat-bottomed boats (the lake is only 10 feet at its deepest) designed to ferry the foreign visitor around the lake on a half day excursion. With both open and enclosed decks, these comfortable boats offer a relaxed way of seeing Tai Lake with its wooded islands and fishing junks. Indeed, many craft ply the lake, some fishing, others carrying people and produce from one shore to another. On a grey day the water seems to merge with the sky, the silhouetted junks apparently suspended between the two. Only as you draw near does the reflection on the glassy water reveal the truth. Land at the Island of Three Hills for a fine panorama of the lake.

Turtle Head Island

This small peninsula, the shape of a turtle's head, juts out into Tai Lake. It is reached over a small arched bridge (Perpetual Spring Bridge). In spring, with both sides lined with cherry trees in full blossom, it is at its most spectacular. Water has been 'borrowed' — a familiar feature of Chinese garden landscapes — from the adjacent Tai Lake to give Turtle Head Island its own small one. The pleasure ground has several pavilions, though its natural beauty and rocky shoreline are its main features. Tai Lake, you will be told, is best seen from Turtle Head Island: indeed the view is splendid both on calm days and in bad weather when, despite the shallowness of the water, quite large waves crash onto the rocks.

Li Garden

Li Garden by Li Lake was constructed in 1929 on the site of a much earlier garden. The main entrance, which is about 20 minutes' walk from Hubin and Shiuxiu Hotels, is through a rock passage which cascades with jasmine. There is also a gate to the garden in front of Hubin Hotel, which is sometimes unlocked for hotel guests. The garden features water and rock conglomerations as well as interesting individual rocks from Tai Lake. For centuries the creators of Chinese gardens have vied amongst themselves to procure the most perfect Tai Lake rocks. An 11th-century catalogue of rocks states that 'the most desirable have tortuous, rugged contours and abundant hollows'. You should be able to see through the rocks, but water must not collect in them. It has been known for selected rocks to be returned to the lake for a further 10 years to improve their contours.

Tai Lake Workers' Sanatorium

Perched on an island, linked by bridge to the northern

banks of the lake, is a workers' sanatorium, the pure air and abundance of fresh food being excellent for convalescence. A visit to the sanatorium can sometimes be arranged for foreign tour groups. Here, in a tranquil spacious setting, visiters may see patients being treated by a combination of western and Chinese methods, including heat treatment with wax and acupuncture.

Plum Tree Garden

On the northern shores of Tai Lake is the Plum Tree, or Mei, Garden. In the Qing Dynasty this was a peach garden, but during this century over 10,000 plum trees of many varieties (for example dragon plum, jade butterfly plum), some scented, have been planted. It is a breathtaking sight in spring.

Xihui Park and Jichang Garden

To the west of the city of Wuxi, between Xi Shan and Hui Shan (*shan* means hill) lies Xihui Park. Within this spacious park are to be found several small gardens, a number of teahouses well patronized by local people, a museum and a pagoda strikingly positioned at the top of Xi Shan.

Jichang Garden This charming, tranquil garden, which lies on the right of the park entrance, is the best known of the gardens in Xihui Park. The layout of Jichang Garden, or the Garden of Ease of Mind, is 16th century, although the pavilions have been extensively restored and extended. Blending the elements of water, rocks and architecture, it provides an excellent example of the traditional Chinese garden. The 18th-century emperor, Qianlong, so enjoyed this garden that he based the design of the Garden of Harmonious Interest upon it. This can be seen today at the Summer Palace, near Peking.

The Second Spring under Heaven From Jichang Garden a short walk further into the park leads to the Second Spring under Heaven. The spring water was graded by Lu Yu, the Tang Dynasty scholar and tea expert, as the 'second best in China' for making tea. Today the spring is overlooked by an attractive, often crowded, teahouse.

Nearby is an interesting garden, featuring Tai Lake rocks, which is mostly Ming, but with earlier and later elements. One small pavilion is said to date from the Qin Dynasty (221-206BC); it has no roof because, the story goes, the head of the family announced that he would not give it one until a family member came first in the civil service examinations.

Municipal Museum Situated to the left of the Xihui Park entrance, the Municipal Museum has some lovely early pottery dating from the foundation of Wuxi and a memorial pavilion to Tai Bo, traditionally said to be the founder of the city of Wuxi.

Hui Shan Clay Figurine Workshop

Making these figurines dates from Ming times when it was discovered that the clay from Hui Shan, the hill to the west of the city, was particularly malleable, very hard when dry and fired well. During the early part of this century the craft was dying, but since 1949 it has once again become a thriving industry producing six million dolls per annum. Traditionally the figurines were of opera characters, but the repertoire has now been greatly expanded to include anything from pandas to figures of Santa Claus. Dough figurines are also produced.

There is an on-the-spot shop where visitors can buy some of the figurines they have seen being produced, and a few interesting display cabinets of some of the earlier work done in Hui Shan clay.

Wuxi's Silk Industry

For some 1500 years, if not more, silk has been produced and woven in the Wuxi area. According to Peregetes, a Greek monk of the first century, 'the Seres (Chinese) make precious garments resembling in colour the flowers of the field and rivalling the work of spiders'.

Today silk is produced much as it always has been. Visitors who come to Wuxi between April and November may be taken to see a commune where silk worms are reared. The miniscule worms that hatch after 10 days spend the next 30 living in bamboo baskets and gorging themselves on mulberry leaves. They are gourmets and will only produce high quality silk if fed *lusang*, the less hardy leafier variety of mulberry: so this problem has been surmounted by grafting *lusang* onto the hardier wild mulberry *yesang*. The worms are then transferred onto inclining straw trays where for five days they spin their cocoons. The best are kept for breeding and within five days they will hatch, mate, lay eggs and die. The remainder are sent to the filature, or silk-reeling, mill.

There are several silk-reeling mills in Wuxi, but it is the

Number One Silk-reeling Mill which is most commonly shown to foreign visitors. The present factory dates from 1933. It now has 1400 workers (80% women) producing some 300 tons of raw silk per annum. Visitors are shown how, on arrival at the factory, the cocoons are first sorted, and soaked in boiling water. The raw silk threads are then drawn up, twisted together and reeled onto small spools which hold silk from four cocoons. On average each cocoon produces 1000 yards of silk. Each girl in the reeling unit at this mill is in charge of 60 little spools. The cocoons bob in trays of water underneath the machine while the girl dashes hither and thither unravelling the start of the cocoon and threading it onto the spool. Next the silk is rereeled onto larger spools combining several threads, and then into large skeins.

Further stages in the silk making process are also shown to foreign visitors. A visit to a weaving mill may be included on a tour itinerary, or to an embroidery factory, where both machine and hand embroidery on silk and other materials are done. Much of the intricately embroidered table and bed linen which is sold in the west comes from this factory.

Excursions from Wuxi

Yixing

To the west of Wuxi, about 1½-hours' drive, is the ancient town of Yixing, which is famous for its beautiful and functional pottery. The first kilns were reputedly set up here during the Spring and Autumn period (770-481BC) by the beauty Xi Shi (a former mistress of the King of Wu), in partnership with a minister from the Kingdom of Yue. Xi Shi had been planted as a spy on the King of Wu by the defeated King of Yue who, when her cover was blown, escaped to Yixing with Minister Fang.

The advantage of this good looking pottery is that in summer tea will not go bad if left in the pot overnight. The pots can be put on a unmasked flame but (unlike Xi Shi) will not become too hot to handle.

Dongshan

In 1981 China International Travel Service plans to inaugurate a trip to the neighbouring mountain Dongshan, west of Wuxi (maybe staying overnight in a guesthouse) to see the temples and tea brigades — here is produced a very expensive tea which takes 60,000 young leaves to make just one catty (approximately 1¼ pounds).

The Grand Canal

A second new trip planned by CITS is a boat journey across Tai Lake and down the Grand Canal to Hangzhou. This will start early in the morning and, with several stops along the way, should arrive in Hangzhou late the same evening.

Recommended Reading

The Chinese Garden by Maggie Keswick (Academy Editions, London, and Rizzoli, New York 1978) is an authoritative, lavishly produced and beautifully illustrated book which gives the reader a close understanding of the history, development and cultural background of this complex subject. *Nagel's Encyclopedia-Guide: China* is always useful, with its wealth of historical information. *Marco Polo: The Travels* (Penguin Books 1958) makes delightful reading. During Marco Polo's years in China (1280s to '90s) he became enamoured with Jiangsu Province and is said to have held a high official post in Yangzhou for three years.

Jiangsu is rich in literary associations, and several major writers are accessible to western readers through translations into English. Li Bai (Li Po), the great Tang poet, believed to have drowned near Nanjing, is well represented. A selection of his poetry appears in *Li Po and Tu Fu*, translated by Arthur Cooper (Penguin Books 1973). Also well worth dipping into is *Honglou Meng*, the outstanding Qing novel about the fall of a great family by Cao Xueqin. The author's family owned and ran the cloud brocade factory in Nanjing. Because Cao's grandfather had lived there, the Humble Administrator's Garden is widely assumed to be the original of Daguan Garden in the story. The most recent complete translation in English is by Yang Hsien-yi and Gladys Yang: *A Dream of Red Mansions* (3 volumes, Foreign Languages Press 1978-80). The novel is also known as *The Story of the Stone*, a title used in David Hawkes's erudite translation, of which three out of five volumes have so far been published (Penguin Books 1973-80).

Cao Xueqin was born towards the end of the reign of Emperor Kangxi, who stayed with the novelist's family four times during his tours of the Yangzi Valley. A fascinating view of court life and the problems of ruling China in the 17th and early 18th centuries, seen through the eyes of the emperor himself, is provided by Jonathan Spence's *Emperor of China: Self-portrait of K'ang-hsi* (Random House 1974, Penguin

Books 1977). For a literary account of life in China in more recent times, Chen Jo-hsi's anthology *The Execution of Mayor Yin and Other Stories,* translated by Nancy Ing and Howard Goldblatt (Indiana University Press 1978) is a subtle portrayal of the Cultural Revolution period. Several of her stories are set in Nanjing.

Lastly, for details on Jiangsu's traditional crafts, Michael Carter's *Crafts of China* (Aldus Books 1977) provides useful information on the subject.

Useful Addresses

Nanjing

Airport
Inquiries tel. 41114
飞机场

Antique Store
7-11 Hangzhong Road, tel. 44550
文物商店　汉中路7-11号

Arts and Crafts Store
168 Xinjiekou
工艺美术品商店　新街口168号

Bank of China
3 Zhongshan Road East, tel. 43336
中国银行　中山东路3号

Civil Aviation Administration of China (CAAC)
76 Zhongshan Road East, tel. 43378
中国民航　中山东路76号

China International Travel Service (CITS)
313 Zhongshan Road North, tel. 86968, 85153
中国国际旅行社　中山北路313号

Foreign Language ᴌookstore
137 Zhongshan Road East, tel. 41881
外文书店　中山东路137号

Friendship Store
3 Daqing Road, tel. 32802
友谊商店　大庆路3号

Jiangsu Art Gallery
266 Changjiang Road, tel. 42884
江苏美术馆　长江路266号

東山詩三百餘首僧得率多寫首應酬
讀者或以為俗語蓋以我為語或以為
色霧藏諸圓隨人目之一見朕尓萬非
語也亦明云修習空花萬行宴坐水月
如二大士者庶幾乎正信調直不離起
不蘭枝上金鳳翔無影樹之王宴圓鏡
無真有有空無有
學者狐疑凈影圓證真如未然有無
否則隨人生解憶無支決此刪而餘之
是為序

雍正十一年癸丑五月朔旦御筆

宣統三年四月江蘇巡撫程德全敬錄

Nanjing Bookstore
Taiping Road South, tel. 42781
南京书店　太平南路

Nanjing Gallery
199 Zhongshan Road
南京图馆　中山路199号

Nanjing Post Office
25 Zhongshan Road, tel. 42338
南京市邮局　中山路25号

Nanjing Railway Station
Shaoshan Road, tel. 34272
南京火车站　韶山路

Nanjing Taxi Company
Beijing Road West Intersection, tel. 33890
南京出租汽车公司　北京西路口

Nanjing West Railway Station
Xiaguan, tel. 85511
南京西火车站　下关

Nanjing University
11 Hankou Road, tel. 34651
南京大学　汉口路11号

Renmin Bazaar
71 Zhongshan Road South, tel. 42766
人民商场　中山南路71号

Telegram Office
8 Youfu Street West, tel. 42435
电信局营业处　游府西街8号

Xinjiekou Department Store
3 Zhongshan Road South, tel. 41300
新街口百货商店　中山南路3号

Zhonghuamen Railway Station
Yuhua Road, tel. 24183
中华门火车站　雨花路

Suzhou

Antique Store
433 Renmin Road, tel. 4972
文物商店　人民路433号

Arts and Crafts Sales Department
Cayuanchang, tel. 6313
工艺美术服务部　察院场

Bank of China
50 Guanqian Street, tel. 6309
中国银行　观前街50号

Caizhizhai Candy Store
Guanqian Street, tel. 3388
采芝斋糖果店　观前街

China International Travel Service (CITS)
115 Youyi Road, tel. 5931
中国国际旅行社　友谊路115号

Daoxiangcun Candy Store
53 Guanqian Street, tel. 3964
稻香村糖果店　观前街53号

Friendship Store
92 Guanqian Street, tel. 4824
友谊商店　观前街92号

Number One Hospital
Shizi Street, tel. 3637
第一医院　十梓街

Paintings and Calligraphy Store
28 Guanqian Street, tel. 5868
古吴轩　观前街28号

Renmin Department Store
Beiju, tel. 3508
人民商场　北局

Suzhou Post Office
Cayuanchang, tel. 3480
苏州邮局营业处　察院场

Suzhou Railway Station
Enquiries tel. 2831
火车站问讯处

Telephone and Telegraph Office
378 Renmin Road, tel. 3030
日夜电报电话营业处　人民路378号

Tourist Taxi Company
271 Youyi Road, tel. 2940
旅遊汽车服务公司　友谊路271号

Xinhua Bookstore
Guanqian Street, tel. 3202
新华书店　观前街

Wuxi

Antique Store
466 Zhongshan Road, tel. 4460
文物商店　中山路466号

Bank of China
168 Renmin Road, tel. 3386
中国银行　人民路168号

China International Travel Service (CITS)
7 Xinsheng Road, tel. 5469
中国国际旅行社　新生路7号

Dongfanghong Department Store
495 Renmin Road, tel. 2362
东方红商场　人民路495号

Friendship Store
8 Zhongshan Road South, tel. 2513
友谊商店　中山南路8号

Number One People's Hospital
111 Renmin Road, tel. 3970
第一人民医院　人民路111号

Wuxi Post Office
230 Renmin Road, tel. 4448
无锡邮局营业处　人民路230号

Wuxi Railway Station
Chezhan Road, tel. 2012
无锡火车站　车站路

Xinhua Bookstore
333 Zhongshan Road, tel. 2363
新华书店　中山路333号

Index of Places

Bell Pavilion 大钟亭 45
Changshu 长熟 74
Cold Mountain Temple 寒山寺 68
Daming Temple 大明寺 53
Dongshan 东山 86
Drum Tower 鼓楼 . . . . : 45
Fifth Spring under Heaven 天下第五泉 54
Flat Hill 平山 53
Flat Hill Residence 平山堂 53
Forest of Lions 狮子林 66
Garden of Joy 怡园 67
Garden of the Master of Fishing Nets 网师园 64
Grand Canal 大运河 26
Historical Museum, Suzhou 苏州博物馆 68
Hui Shan 惠山 84
Hui Shan Clay Figurine Workshop 惠山泥人厂 85
Humble Administrator's Garden 拙政园 64
Jian Zhen Memorial Hall 鉴真纪念堂 54
Jichang Garden 寄畅园 84
Li Garden 蠡园 82
Lingering Garden 留园 65
Linggu Temple Park 灵谷寺公园 42
Lingyan Hill 灵岩山 71
Memorial Hall of the Delegates of
    the Chinese Communist Party 中共代表会纪念堂 45
Ming Tomb 明孝陵 39
Mochou Lake 莫愁湖 48
Municipal Museum, Wuxi 无锡博物馆 85
Museum of the Taiping Heavenly Kingdom 太平天国历史
    陈列馆 44
Nanjing Museum 南京博物院 45
Nanjing University 南京大学 48
Northern Pagoda 北塔 68
Number One Silk-reeling Mill 第一缫丝厂 86
Observatory 天文台 42
Pavilion of the Waves 沧浪亭 65
People's Revolutionary Martyrs' Memorial 革命先烈纪念碑 43
Plum Tree Garden 梅园 84
Precious Belt Bridge 宝带桥 68
Purple Gold Mountains 紫金山 31
Qianlong Boathouse and Pier 乾隆之码头 53

Qixia Temple 栖霞寺 49
Rain Flower Terrace 雨花台 43
Ruins of the Ming Palace 明古宫遗址 44
Second Spring under Heaven 天下第二泉 84
Sky Flat Mountain 天平山 71
Slender West Lake 瘦西湖 52
Stone Carvings of the Southern Dynasties 南朝大型石刻 . . . 43
Sun Yat-sen Mausoleum 中山陵 39
Suzhou Embroidery Research Institute 苏州刺绣研究所 72
Suzhou Sandalwood Fan Factory 苏州扇厂 72
Tai Lake 太湖 81
Tai Lake Workers' Sanatorium 工人太湖疗养院 82
Tiger Hill 虎丘 70
Turtle Head Island 鼋头渚 82
West Garden Temple 西园寺 67
Xi Shan 锡山 84
Xihui Park 锡惠公园 84
Xuanwu Park 玄武湖公园 48
Yangzhou 扬州 52
Yangzhou Museum 扬州博物馆 53
Yangzi River Bridge 长江大桥 42
Yixing 宜兴 86
Zhonghua Gate 中华门 46

Qianlong boathouse, Yangzhou

Chronology of Periods in Chinese History

Palaeolithic	c.600,000-7000BC
Neolithic	c.7000-1600BC
Shang	c.1600-1027BC
Western Zhou	1027-771BC
Eastern Zhou	770-256BC
Spring and Autumn Annals	722-481BC
Warring States	480-221BC
Qin	221-206BC
Former (Eastern) Han	206BC-25AD
Later (Western) Han	25-220
Three Kingdoms	220-265
Western Jin	265-316
Northern and Southern Dynasties	317-589
Sui	589-618
Tang	618-907
Five Dynasties and Ten Kingdoms	907-960
Northern Song	960-1127
Southern Song	1127-1279
Jin	1115-1234
Yuan (Mongol)	1279-1368
Ming	1368-1644
Qing (Manchu)	1644-1911
Republic	1911-1949
People's Republic	1949-

(Following page) Suzhou canal scene